STUDENT VIOLENCE

By Edward Bloomberg

Public Affairs Press, Washington, D. C.

About the Author

Edward Bloomberg is an Assistant Professor of French literature at the University of California at Davis. He holds A.B. and Ph.D. degrees from Yale University. While pursuing graduate studies at Yale he was a Carnegie Teaching Fellow and an Honorary Woodrow Wilson Fellow.

Copyright 1970 by Public Affairs Press
419 New Jersey Avenue, S.E., Washington, D. C.

Printed in the United States of America
Library of Congress Catalog Card No. 70-133450

INTRODUCTION

Members of the committee on student unrest recently appointed by President Nixon can read this book with considerable benefit. It is far more insightful than any other book on the subject.

Unlike those academicians who have written learned but ambiguous treatises about the turmoil on our campuses, Prof. Bloomberg doesn't pull any punches. He places much of the blame where it rightfully belongs—with those professors and college administrators who have abdicated their responsibilities by permitting and even encouraging students to "do their thing" with little or no regard for the consequences.

In these pages, Prof. Bloomberg forthrightly discusses how and why many college professors have in effect been permissive in their reactions toward student demonstrations that have led to violence. They are, he contends, so unsure of their values, so dominated by moral-relativism, that they can barely distinguish between validity and absurdity.

Prof. Bloomberg does not, of course, relieve left-wing students of their responsibility. He has no brief for their mindless crusade against our educational institutions. He denounces their resort to violence as the equivalent of unreasoning anti-intellectualism. What he says in this regard is in large part confirmed by my own observations during visits to leading colleges in the past few years. I have repeatedly seen and heard many things similar to those he mentions in these pages.

To truly understand the radicalization of the young it is necessary, I believe, to take into account the extent to which depersonalization of our institutions of higher education has contributed to the atmosphere of frustration felt by many young people. The author alludes to this but I wish he had gone into it in some depth.

Still, a short volume such as this cannot make all the stops along the way. What matters most of all is that Prof. Bloomberg has written a cogent plea for reason at a time when the voices of sanity on our campuses are muted. Hopefully, this book will give those voices the encouragement to speak up.

ALLAN C. BROWNFELD

CONTENTS

1

CAUSES

Few people approve of campus violence, but fewer still understand it. Some accept the explanation of those committing the violence: our society is corrupt; the university has sold what little soul it had to the military-industrial complex; an overwhelming majority of Americans are racist pigs. Others suspect that communist plotters have cleverly blended equal amounts of long hair, marijuana, and pornography to compose a poison lethal to American ways. Still others, who should know better, blame the Oedipus complex, the refusal of "society" to give responsibility to America's youth, or the supposedly marginal position which students occupy in the social structure.

To establish absolute causality in such a matter is beyond human intelligence. It is possible, however, to offer a series of hypotheses less likely to collapse upon the most cursory examination than the porcine nature of capitalists or the scheming ways of Marxists.

Among the causes which will be discussed here are the radical's opinion of human nature, the professor's character, and the sanctification of sloppy thinking. I shall attempt to show how these foster anti-rationalism, "absolute" relativism, Marxism, and existentialism, all of which lead, in turn, to the illogical demands of student radicals and to violence.

To decide what sort of society man deserves and is capable of maintaining, one must discover his moral nature. Is man good, bad, or both? Are all men equally good, or are there basic differences among groups of men (races) and/or among individuals in the same group? A person's answers to these questions, whether consciously asked or not, determine his politics.

A brief examination of the positions taken in the past and their consequences will enable us to judge the radical's idea of human nature.

Most Catholic thinkers of the Middle Ages, the early Calvinists, and the Jansenists of seventeenth century France held that man is almost completely evil. He is a fallen being who, without God's help, is absolutely incapable of doing, or even desiring, good. His natural reward in the after-life is hell. Heaven is reserved for the minority to whom God has decided, for reasons of his own, to accord grace. Good deeds and thoughts on earth come exclusively from this unmerited divine favor.

A rival current of Christian thought, declared heretical in 418, starts with Pelagius. Man is naturally good. He is capable of gaining salvation by himself, through his own merit. God's intervention is not necessary. This tradition, promulgated by the Jesuits, has survived and is dominant in both Catholic and Protestant thought today.

During the Renaissance the idea of man's inherent goodness separated from theology and began to hold sway in secular thought. Nevertheless, it had its enemies. They objected that one had only to open one's eyes to see that evil was done by men every day. Jean-Jacques Rousseau popularized a corollary to the theory of man's goodness which answered this objection: all that is evil in man comes, not from his nature, but from society. If society changed for the better, he would no longer sin. Thus was born the cult of revolution in the name of morality. Among the community's "corrupt institutions," property was singled out as especially vicious. According to Rousseau, the first man who aeons ago seized a piece of land and cried out, "This is mine" was responsible for evil. Rousseau never told why (although the "depraved" habit of thinking seems to have been involved) that first good and uncorrupted individual was so grasping; the idea of a human nature less than perfect was carefully eschewed.

Have either of these concepts worked to man's advantage? The "man is evil" school of thought has produced dictatorship and easy slaughter. Why spare man, why respect him, if he is, by nature, scum? Punishment is what he needs. What holders of this theory must explain, however, is how it applies to themselves. If they too are evil, why should they escape the lash? Why should they oppress their equals? When rulers did not need to consider world opinion—they had no fear of punishment— the answer was very simple: "Why not?" More recently, it has become necessary to justify oneself. "I can oppress because I am not man, but superman," was the obvious answer. I can oppress because I am not common, but noble; not Jew, but Aryan; not black, but white. The theory of man's inherent evil leads, in the modern world, where people reflect on these questions, to its own denial: "man" is split into two races, one of which remains evil, while the other is promoted to higher status. The *reductio ad absurdum*—man is no longer man, but men— demolishes the theory.

The idea of man's goodness has brought forth nothing better. Its direct result was the French Revolution, which recognized Rousseau as its spiritual leader. It was characterized by the same slaughter and the same absence of human liberties which were the result of the idea that man is evil. The difference was not in deeds but in words. The French Revolution left us many elevated sentiments and gestures. It also left us mountains of corpses and the dictatorship of Napoleon. The results of the Russian Revolution are equally discouraging. If the theory of man's goodness were sound, surely its application would not produce evil. It therefore seems difficult to avoid the conclusion that the idea is false.

If humanity were pragmatic, it would have collectively abandoned both these theories as unconducive to government permitting people to do as they wish. The two ideas have not died, of course. They have shared the stage since the eighteenth century, subjecting man to the same deprivation, fear, and slavery. Man is now evil in Spain, in Greece, and in most of South America. He is being punished for it. Man is good—or at least he would be if property had not corrupted him—in the U.S.S.R., in China, in Hungary, in Albania, in Poland, and in Czechoslovakia. One suspects, however, that the inhabitants of these countries have not achieved the perfection necessary to accept with equanimity the loss of liberty, the torture, and the hardships which have been inflicted upon them.

A third view of man's moral make-up has come into favor in

a few countries in the last two hundred years. It is an obvious, inelegant, petty bourgeois solution: man is that creature your grocer would tell you he is, a mixture of good and evil, reason and madness, love and hate. Whoever ignores one side of his nature steps into monstrosity: "He who tries to be an angel becomes a beast." Some people at every period in history have, of course, known this. But it is with Montesquieu, J. S. Mill, and the American Founding Fathers, especially James Madison, that man's mixed moral nature is applied to questions of polity. The American Revolution and the American system of government are founded on it. They presuppose that man will be good only when watched by others, only when threat of punishment exists, only when he knows that he cannot have all the power to himself. Governments, made up of men, must be equally subject to controls. On the other hand, man is capable of governing himself, provided he takes his weaknesses into account when fixing upon a form of government. He has a limited, but real, sense of fair play. Most important, he is worth the trouble it takes to organize a system which will not degenerate into despotism.

In economic matters, the applications are obvious. Self-interest plays a substantial, if not a predominant, role in the life of man. He will work harder for himself than for the commonweal. The best incentive to production is therefore the hope of realizing a profit. What is referred to as free enterprise is the result. If, however, man is allowed to pursue his self-interest without any rules, arbiters, or threats of punishment, he will destroy his competitors; hence the need for laws governing commerce and penalties for violators.

Man's conduct in economic, social, and political matters will be most beneficial to others when restrained by law. Law will be most beneficial when restrained by the vote. The vote must be kept honest by laws which permit people of all factions to supervise the casting and counting of ballots. If there were no goodness in man, this system would fail, for men judge at every step. If there were no evil, checks and balances would be superfluous. A Soviet-type regime would be more successful. Judging from the results, the American idea of human nature would seem to be right.

Since the two extremes of depraved and angelic man have been avoided in America, the debate has traditionally been based on more subtle distinctions. Is man 40% evil and 60% good or vice versa? Conservatives see 60% evil, liberals see only 40%. This explains their respective positions regarding the size to which government can grow without becoming dangerous and the role of incentive in the economy. The tendency has usually been toward moderation and tolerance, for both sides realize that they are dealing, not with black and white, but with shades of gray.

How do the two spearhead associations of youthful radicalism—SDS (Students for a Democratic Society) and BSU (Black Students Unions)—fit into this framework? SDS theology clearly states that man is thoroughly good. It puts all the blame for evil on society. This sad repeat of Rousseau's error leads its followers to the conclusion that our society must be destroyed at any cost. SDS supporters are not exactly consistent when they refer to all who participate in the American system, especially the enforcers of its laws, as "pigs." Logically, they too should be seen as victims of society rather than perpetrators of evil. This contradiction points up one of the strangest aberrations of the SDS: they arrive at two humanities, the good "people" and the evil "pigs," in the fashion of those who believe man is evil. This permits them to treat "pigs" as totalitarians treat the general population. Since, in fact, practically all Americans do fit into the pig category (most of us favor the system and own property), most of us are only getting what we deserve when we are treated violently. Pigs "should be put in pig pens," as SDS members are wont to say. Love becomes hate, and utopia becomes a concentration camp.

The various Black Students Unions are less doctrinaire and less versed in revolutionary literature. Nevertheless, they have to a certain extent swallowed the SDS explanation and adopted the same bastard mixture of "all men are good" and "some are good but others are 'pigs'." They adhere, for the most part, to the SDS doctrine that the swine—their opponents—can be suppressed by any means.

It can be concluded that the first cause of campus violence is the acceptance by the two most revolutionary student groups of an especially virulent form of a theory of man's nature which has always, even in its most benign forms, led to violence—and, eventually, to totalitarianism.

As a professor, it is painful for me to speak ill of my colleagues. The remarks that follow perhaps should have been buried with me, as befits family secrets. It is impossible to understand student violence, however, without a forthright discussion of the professor's personal characteristics. All professors are not, of course, the same. But a large number have fairly similar characteristics that cannot—or, at least, should not—be ignored.

One conspicuous professorial characteristic is the absence of that combination of ambition and aggressiveness which is generally called strength. In our society, still hard-working and competitive, college teaching is a relaxed and uncompetitive profession. The zealous seek much more remunerative positions. Those who wish to avoid the rigors of business, law, and medicine seek refuge in the university. This arrangement should be to everyone's satisfaction: havens are provided for those who do not wish to compete, and society procures the services of intelligent people at relatively low wages.

Some (first and foremost the professors themselves) would dispute the application of the adjective "relaxed" to college teaching. Have not academic sociologists made studies showing that the average professor works fifty-three hours a week? They proceed thus: questionnaires are sent to the professors asking how many hours they spend teaching, consulting, reading, writing, and meeting each week. They then simply compile the results, which prove only that professors think—or say—they work many hours. Sociologists call this "scientific research." (A truly scientific study would be based on observation rather than hearsay. As it would require electronic spying, one would suppose that it falls into the category of impossible research.) They include the time spent counting answers as some of their own hard work. The point they miss is, of course, that it is precisely because professors have such a relaxed life that they consider chatting and reading to be herculean tasks.

Professors would even more strenuously contest the assertion that college teaching is noncompetitive. For years they have been talking about the dog-eat-dog world of publish-or-perish. While it is true that they will be removed from the forty or fifty most important universities if they do not publish within their first eight years of teaching, it is not true that they must publish in great quantity. Nor is it true that they must publish works of high quality. They are *not* competing against other works on their subjects. They are merely obliged to treat some subject or other. This is especially true at present, for there are many more jobs than there are reasonably competent people to fill them.

The fact that some professors do have nervous breakdowns proves not that they are involved in a rat race but that even a small degree of tension is too much for them. In times of trouble, the consequences of this weakness can be ruinous. The professor has chosen a life of reflection, not of action. He has no desire for acrimonious debate, excitement, or violence. He has entered teaching to get away from all that. It would be hard to find a person worse equipped to defend himself against intransigence, fanaticism, and violence.

At the bottom of his weakness is something akin to a feeling of inadequacy. The professor is not going to admit this any more than anybody else, but he knows it. Scholarly children with glasses are usually not the most popular in elementary schools. It is difficult for the young to esteem themselves if others do not. Inferiority feelings breed an insatiable need of reassurance that one is not inferior. The professor consequently has a greater need of popularity ("compensatory approval," a psychologist would say) in later life than the average person. The result can be close conformity to what he believes to be the values of his social group. The prospect of encountering disapproval is frequently sufficient to silence the professor who feels himself to be in the minority. In those few professors who were radically crippled by unpopularity in their youths (they often take up sociology and psychology in order to discover how to be liked and later become professors in these subjects), the desire for approval can become so intense that they become radicals themselves. In this way they are surrounded by noisy approbation (those who disapprove are more polite) and almost forget their sad secret. By conforming to the values they attribute to students, they come to think of themselves as nonconformists or rebels. Consequently, unlike most professors, they come to relish turmoil. This loud and irrational minority suffering from acute inferiority feelings can tend to dominate the majority of conformists with lesser psychic lesions. If two radicals manage to speak first at a faculty meeting, the others assume them to be the majority, and act accordingly. Those decisions of faculty senates which are so shockingly foolish as to be incomprehensible to outsiders are almost always the result of such pressures. Student rationality is hardly encouraged by these irrational decrees.

Another reason for the average professor's reluctance to speak out is his specialist's modesty. He recognizes that he is qualified to speak only of his own field of inquiry. He feels that others are surely more competent than he on all other matters. This commendable characteristic is unfortunately additional prompting to irrationality. Madness shouts while reason hides. The students conclude that reason and madness are one.

In addition, the professor does not really spend his evenings thinking about how a university should be run, about how peace and justice can be combined, about how students should be educated. He has other interests and does not really want to be bothered with questions of policy. But neither does he want to be bossed about by administrators. In the past few decades he has consequently taken onto himself the essential policy-making powers in the university. There is thus very little which he can, in good faith, blame on the administration. The 25 per cent of professors who attend policy meetings decide almost every issue. When someone in favor of a new procedure announces that it has been adopted at X college, the professor, who has no idea what should be done, says to himself: "They must have thought it out at X college. Why should we be different?" Weakness, inferiority, specialist's modesty, and indifference all push him towards conformity with X college. This is why a bad program adopted by one university will often be accepted elsewhere.

As if these defects did not suffice to make the professor

something of a collaborationist, he actually agrees with the student radicals on some of the issues, most of which are reducible to a condemnation of the "American way of life." The merits of these issues will be discussed later. What it is necessary to understand now is that from the character of the American professor it is easy to deduce his attitude toward American society. His ego is constantly pricked by the larger public. He cannot help comparing his position in the pecking order with that of his colleagues from other countries. In France and Germany, few have more prestige than "Monsieur le professeur " or "Herr Professor." The little people of these countries bow obsequiously to professors, and literati make politics. While in America prominent businessmen are the most respected, in Europe the professor, the journalist, the writer—the intellectuals—are considered the ultimate sources of wisdom.

This difference in prestige is paralleled (and partially caused) by different pay scales. Although the American professor is the best paid in the world on an absolute scale, he receives less, relatively, than scholars in other countries. Whereas in the U.S.S.R., that worker's paradise, a professor earns three times more than a skilled worker, in the United States their pay is approximately equal. Our market economy has placed a lower value on the professor than any statist nation. Despite the lip service he pays to egalitarianism, this irks him. It is confirmation of that inferiority he senses in himself. He is therefore predisposed to critiques of the country which treats him so badly, especially to those that come from Europe, where a learned man is treated with considerable respect. It is not surprising that he accepts in part the anti-American, anti-capitalistic theories which are unquestioned dogma in European intellectual circles. The prestige of "European ideas," a vestige of our colonial days, is an additional factor in the equation.

Traditional America (i.e., before the New Deal) and most of contemporary America look upon government as an institution designed to assure public tranquility and protect individual rights. It has no greater purpose. Salvation and the discovery of the meaning of life are left to each man. For the traditionalist there are two good reasons for this. First, he is afraid of a government large enough to solve all of life's problems. He thinks that power corrupts and that in having his metaphysics solved by the government he would lose his basic rights. He enjoys citing examples of the loss of freedom elsewhere. Second, he usually has some belief or other which gives his life meaning. He is convinced that no government is better at solving metaphysical problems than he. The traditional American is, as one can see, a cocky little fellow, hopelessly outmoded.

The European picture of politics is something entirely different. The opinion-makers of Europe, the "leftist intellectuals," feel that politics should not be concerned with petty procedural, legalistic, hair-splitting nonsense about individual rights and the extent of government power. No government in France, for example (and governments of every stripe have been in power over the last three hundred years), has granted *habeas corpus,* or clearly established the principle that the accused is innocent until proven guilty, or created a judiciary free from political influence.

"Freedom" has its possibilities as a slogan in Europe, but usually means freedom from the preceding government, from another conquering government, or from "American imperialism." It is freedom for the *nation,* not for the individual.

The purpose of politics in European intellectual debate is rather to give the individual a system, not too incoherent, which will function as a religion. Marxist explanations, for example, are total ones, covering every aspect of life. One cannot cut off a segment and say, "Here is a nonpolitical matter; here is a personal matter." There are no such things. The struggle between classes explains one's sentiments, which are usually manifestations of bourgeois upbringing . Crime, *états d'âme,* religious questioning and belief, metaphysics and epistemology, racial prejudice, and sexual aberration are all the result of class society. In fact, concern with individual liberties is bourgeois tomfoolery. A government influenced by such thinking is therefore not concerned with establishing or preserving rights, but rather with applying its theology to all.

The average American professor is lodged between European and American tradition. He supports individual rights, but he wants government to be more than a keeper of the peace. His lack of confidence in himself prevents him from believing, with the traditional American, that he can find salvation all by himself. He craves for an all-inclusive system in which he could lose his individuality. He is skeptical and fearful of governments unsympathetic to him, but does not share the American fear of government in general. In this he is illogical, for his ideas are based, not on the activities of all-powerful governments, but on those of the American government. To decide whether power corrupts, one should look, not at a weak, but a powerful government. As long as American government is limited, it is usually on the obvious (to most) "right" side of major social issues. Professors, predisposed in this direction by their character, deduce that it should be more powerful in order to do more good. If one accepts the principle that all organisms try to perpetuate themselves and grow, however, one can look upon the commendable past acts of government as predictable strategy: what better way is there to gain power than to convince of its goodness? The truth is perhaps even simpler: power corrupts, but limited power corrupts only the limited. Therefore a limited government can be a force for good. An unchecked one cannot.

From this, a person completely unsympathetic towards academics might conclude that their conduct vis-à-vis radicals is calculated to urge them on to greater demagoguery and violence. An analysis based exclusively on self-interest could corroborate this view. Under a socialistic (i.e., more powerful) government, the professor would have a higher standing. (Supposedly some such system would be instituted by student revolutionaries.) For the present, the more universities are in the headlines, the more important and the more powerful he becomes.

The truth, however, is less flamboyant. The professor is much less interested in headlines than he is appalled by violence. He fears, however, that by unequivocally saying so, he will cause that violence to be visited upon himself. He therefore compromises by declaring that perfectly ridiculous stands on issues are valid, but that violence must be foresworn.

Many people will object to these generalizations because "you can't generalize," a statement which is itself a generalization. If one can't generalize, it is not true. There is, of course, nothing inherently wrong with generalizing. Most human knowledge, in fact, depends upon it. The test of a generalization's validity is its ability to explain specific cases. Three will be given here.

In an article that appeared in *Time* on May 16, 1969, the following was reported: "At the University of Wisconsin 35 senior professors have anonymously formed a group that was instrumental in gathering overwhelming faculty support for the administration's stand against Negro demands for a separate, autonomous Black Studies department . . ." The article is rare in that it portrays professors resisting foolish demands rather than caving in to' them. Even here, however, their tremulous disposition is made overwhelmingly plain by the word "anonymous." Surely the impact on students undecided on the matter and seeking guidance would have been greater had these gentlemen given their names.

In June, 1969, the author of "Law and Order," a weekly feature of the *Davis Enterprise,* a California newspaper, made the following delirious statement in his column: "[colleges] have effectively screened out . . . blacks, spanish-speaking [sic] and other undesirables by awarding them low grades regardless of ability and regardless of actual achievement." When one considers that there are programs for screening blacks who do not meet objective requirements *into* colleges in most American universities today, it becomes plain that this is blatant nonsense. In the community of Davis this newspaper is read by almost everyone, and letters to the editor are common. Yet not one professor rebutted this accusation of professorial racism. The fear of getting into a fight and being accused of defending the Establishment was evidently greater than the love of truth or fair play. The uninformed must have assumed that the writer was stating a reasonable opinion. The encouragement to violence is plain: if racist acts were perpetrated by university professors and no redress were possible, a legitimate case for violence could, indeed, be made.

On May 29, 1969, the *Enterprise* reported the proceedings of a meeting of the Academic Senate of the University of California at Davis. The topic on the floor was a march to Berkeley in favor of a "People's Park." Civil disobedience, one death and several injuries had already occurred.

The leaders of the People's Park movement were radicals with no sense of fair play or legal procedures. Their basic thesis was that people (i.e., radicals) were more important than property, from which they deduced in curious fashion that they could take over property by force (even if they killed some people).

"Although virtually [all the professors] agreed that the possibility of violence occurring was likely indeed, there was a marked split in the senate as to whether it made any sense to urge students not to participate, since, as some faculty noted, a resolution would have little or no effect on individuals' decisions." Here we see that basic inferiority which assumes that at bottom a professor's word has little weight. One professor took the position that any professorial urgings would be "irrelevant." Another went further still and affirmed that "it would be inappropriate for the senate to act like a parent."

Although radical professors spoke in favor of marching, the moderates did not emit reasoned counsel to students desirous of it because, ostensibly, this would somehow be a claim to wisdom superior to that of the students! When one considers that a university is a place where people who admit ignorance— students—go to learn from those who claim knowledge and supposedly at least a small measure of wisdom, the situation was indeed surprising. Astonishingly, the chairman of the senate's committee on educational policy took the position that "the collective wisdom of the senate may well be less than that of any one person." Here we have professorial humility at its most touching.

There is, of course, an excellent reason why the Academic Senate should have made no recommendation regarding the march on Berkeley in favor of a "People's Park": the university is not in politics. But no one mentioned this. The Academic Senate had already made political pronouncements on this very issue! It had voted support for the chancellor who had made a political statement in favor of those who had seized the park and against the "violence" of policemen who had resisted an attempt to seize it a second time. It will be seen

later why the university should make no declarations about
public policy. If it does, however, they may as well be reasonable. Instead, the moderate majority dared not speak up
against the radical minority or even be seen voting against
them! In this connection, it is interesting to note that professors often vote more radically at meetings where there is a
show of hands than by anonymous mail ballot.

The importance of the professor's nature as a precondition
of violence cannot be overestimated. The great majority of
students still feel that the professor knows more than they and
is wiser. Students are constantly asking their professors what
they "should" think about every issue. And—unfortunately—
they do not want to be told to think for themselves. They want
an opinion, a guide. It is because the guide often seems to agree
with the radical that the average student takes radicalism
seriously.

It is difficult to obey laws and moral injunctions in which one
has no faith. It is almost as difficult to observe rules with which
one agrees but which are not absolute. As recently as twenty
years ago the terms "absolute" and "relative" had fairly clear
meanings. "Thou shalt not kill" was an injunction of absolute
value except in certain cases—war and self-defense. It was because of the exceptions that the commandment could be called
"relative." The meaning has changed: relative morality now
means, if anything, that in *every* situation, a given act is of
relative value. Nothing, in other words, can ever in *any* circumstances, be absolutely condemned. Violence is no exception.

This meaning has probably come into existence by analogy
with the adjective "relative" applied to truth. It is generally
accepted by non-thinkers that, as far as truth is concerned,
"everything is relative." This is pure tommyrot, of course, for
if all truths are relative, what do we make of the proposition
"Everything is relative?" If it is relative, there is no reason
to believe it. If it is absolute, it is the proof that everything is
not relative. Stated another way, if there is no absolute truth,
the proposition "There is no absolute truth" is not absolutely
true. Therefore there is an absolute truth—to wit, the proposition

stating that there is none. It is, in fact, the notion of relative truth which is absurd. Absoluteness is implied by the definition of "truth"—viz., that which is, that which corresponds to reality. What possible meaning, for example, could the statement, "It is relatively true that Socrates is mortal," have? If the proposition is not absolutely true, it is plainly false.

The new idea of relative good is equally absurd. Relative to what is a "relatively good" act good? If one answers that it is to be judged by another relative good, the question can be repeated for that good, ad infinitum, until one of two things happens: either an absolute good is named, or it is admitted that the very terms good and evil are bereft of meaning.

Nevertheless, absolute relativism is the fashion right now. Few intellectuals would be prepared to defend anything as absolutely true or absolutely good. The result is that many feel— without knowing precisely why—that nothing can be really *false* or *evil*. Therefore nothing is absolutely forbidden.

In liberal rhetoric, the primary formant of today's youth and the obviously dominant moral influence of the last thirty years, much reference is made to this relative good. It is in its name that most liberal political programs are advertised. It says, "You shall have medicare, or pedicare," but never, "You shall *not* do this," or "You shall not do that." This good is not a creature made to awe us but a doting parent. It loves us and spoils us. If it should turn against us at some important moment, if it should interfere in the slightest way with our whims, we can always say, "You are really nothing at all," or more politely, "Is there not a tribe in Zunbaigi which does as I do?" Relativism is thus permission to commit violence.

The terms good and evil are used as often as before they became relative. Radical students might on the surface be seen as reasonable people aware of the fallacies of relativism. Are not their moral pronouncements always of an absolute and unyielding nature? In fact, however, the only relationship between the relativism of the larger society and the absolutism (i.e., dogmatism) of the radicals is that the former encourages the latter. The relativism of adults prevents them from condemning any behavior at all, even their own vilification. Students are thus free to follow their own inclinations wherever they lead.

Whether this is beneficial or not must be determined by our opinion of man's moral nature. If man is basically good, as radicals contend, no restraints or sanctions are needed. If he is not, the removal of all interdictions can only lead to violence and other outrages.

From this it can be seen that there are certain ideas in the mental landscape which create conditions suitable for the growth of violence. Yet these conditions never determine that violence will occur. Before a tendency becomes an act, people must give their consent. The best defense against predispositions is thought. If we think clearly and wish to do what is right, we will withhold consent. Certain of the ideas prevalent today, however, seem to be not only the result of sloppy thinking, but inevitable causes of new sloppy thinking. Such notions as relative good and relative truth are so self-contradictory and fuzzy that it is impossible simultaneously to understand and believe them. (If one understands that the proposition "Everything is relative" is relative, how can one believe it?) A contradictory idea which becomes current usually does more mischief than a clear one, no matter how evil. Since one cannot understand a contradiction, one renounces comprehension in favor of mystic complicity with a foolish refrain. Thought becomes "irrelevant," and the predisposition to violence goes unchecked.

The way in which past sloppy thinking encourages future sloppy thinking is illustrated by present-day ideas on the subject of tolerance. When a man holds an opinion to be true, but is nevertheless willing to let others disagree, he is tolerant. The "tolerance" of the relativist, firmly ensconced in his illogic, is another matter. Holding no opinion to be true, he accepts all statements as equally gratuitous. When discussing an issue, he says, "I feel that . . . ." or, "It seems to me that . . ." He never attempts to use logic to refute another's opinion or to defend his. All man can do, according to him, is "express" himself. He can make no claim to truth. In the name of what would he do so? He must therefore place side by side as equals authoritarianism and reason, intolerance and tolerance, good and evil, absolutism and relativism. This is a perfect formula for the elimination of all tolerance, because it has no criterion for refuting intolerance (or evil, or violence). It is thus not surprising that relativists rear, along with new relativists, an occasional dogmatic and intolerant youngster. The relativistic parent's humble admission of utter fallibility sets the stage for his radical son's claim of infallibility.

The implications for the university and the state are quite frightening. Infallible people can be ruthless: the fascist and communist systems have always maintained their infallibility as an article of faith and have used it to suppress dissent. Why discuss things if truth comes from authority? Debate implies that truth comes from the use of reason. This is why Black Power leaders and SDS spokesmen do not really discuss. Herbert Marcuse, radical guru extraordinary, has gone so far as to suggest, in a sort of updated *Mein Kampf,* the silencing (by any means necessary) of those who do not agree with his own sloppy thinking.[1] Those in favor of national defense and capitalism and against medicare, increased social security, and other *right* programs should not be allowed to assemble or speak out. Indeed, the schools should systematically brainwash their pupils to avoid wrong thought.[2] Why not, if the way to truth is authoritarianism? Why not, if the larger society has decided that intolerance is just as defensible as tolerance, since it believes everything to be relative?

Practice has followed theory very closely. Why let a lecturer speak in favor of South African policies when they are wrong? Radicals at the University of Wisconsin did not. Why let a South Vietnamese minister speak if he is wrong? Radicals at New York University did not. Why let people read books in which imperialistic lies are to be found? Radicals at George Washington University invaded the Institute for Sino-Soviet Studies and destroyed books. People left to themselves might use reason and sense experience to find truth. Such wrong methods would inevitably lead to wrong answers.

---

[1] Marcuse, Herbert, "Repressive Tolerance," in Wolff, *A Critique of Pure Tolerance.* Beacon Press.

[2] Marcuse, *op.cit.,* pp. 100-101.

Reason is the most dangerous enemy of such enlighteners of mankind. To understand the "thoughts" of an SDS speaker or a Marcuse is to discover one contradiction after another. If reason prevails, they are laughable. If, however, they manage to destroy the idea that reason is valid, they escape the criticism they deserve. Naturally, then, reason is in low repute with the New Left.

It is relativism and its result, authoritarianism, which have given reason such a bad name. In relativism there is no truth. How, therefore, can reason, as it claims, discover truth? In authoritarianism truth is absolute, but only authority can discover it. As there will inevitably be a conflict between authority and reason, the former rejects the latter.

Sloppy thinking (e.g., relativism) destroys reason. Without reason, thinking becomes more sloppy. Indeed the term "thinking" has no meaning without reason, whose three major laws are aptly named the laws of thought. These are identity, excluded middle, and non-contradiction. The law of identity states that a thing is itself (A equals A). This should not be very controversial. The law of excluded middle states that between the truth or falsity of a *simple* proposition (statement) there is no middle ground (A equals B or does not equal B). For example, 2 plus 2 equal 4 or 2 plus 2 do not equal 4. It must be one or the other. There is nothing between the two propositions. The law of non-contradiction states that two contradictory propositions cannot be simultaneously true (A cannot equal B at the same time that A does not equal B). Water, for example, cannot at the same time be a liquid and not be a liquid. A man cannot be simultaneously mortal and immortal.

These three laws taken together are the essence of reason. Deduction (A is greater than B. B is greater than C. Therefore A is greater than C.) is reducible to these laws. All dictionary definitions of reason imply them. They are that definition which subsumes all the others. To deny reason's validity is to say that identity, excluded middle, and non-contradiction are false laws. Thus when an advocate against reason says something, we must assume that he also means the opposite (contradiction). When he says A, he does not mean A (non-identity). How then can there be any thought?

There can oly be rantings. Yet has not Gandhi (an *authority*) said that only a petty man cannot abide a contradiction? By that I suppose he *also* meant the opposite (it is *not* only a petty man who cannot abide a contradiction) since without the law of non-contradiction the opposite of every statement is contained in it.

One cannot reasonably expect the demise of reason to have pleasant consequences. If it is by reason that man differs from the beasts, it follows that irrational man is a beast. Man's nature is partly tribalistic and superstitious. It is the rational part of the mixture which prevents him from being a savage and a fanatic believer in things untrue. It is thus not surprising that the young radical liberated from reason belongs to a violent, primitive, and fanatical tribe, ready to strike out in any way against its enemies. It is not surprising that young radicals claim they are seeking individualism, but end up in tribes which require absolute conformity. Only through the use of reason could they see the contradiction between their words and their deeds.

Their defense against such logical criticism is the denial of the law of non-contradiction. This denial leads to the end of all discourse and consequently to unchecked reliance upon "feeling." Situation ethics and the teeny cliché about doing one's thing are the result. If it feels good, it is good. When one considers that the heroes of the Marquis de Sade were great doers of their own thing, as were Hitler and Stalin, it is difficult to look upon the destruction of reason as a step towards moral perfection.

The radical denial of the law of non-contradiction is, of course, absurd. For proof we need only apply this theory to itself (two contradictory statements *can* be true). "I deny the law of non-contradiction," says our irrationalist. We caution him that without it he is simultaneously saying that he accepts the law of non-contradiction. He has two choices. He can deny that we are right: "Deny and accept are opposites, I don't *accept*, I *deny*." In that case he recognizes the law of non-contradiction in virtue of which acceptance and denial are not one and the same. His original assertion was ridiculous. Or he can agree with us: "I accept and deny the law of non-contradiction simultaneously." In this case we ask him what this law, which he now accepts, says. The answer is that it denies the possibility of accepting contradiction. He must therefore eliminate contradiction in order to live up to his original statement (the denial of the law of non-contradiction). He is left with non-contradiction. It is therefore impossible to deny the law of non-contradiction.

Radicals who deny reason must nevertheless speak in daily life in order to make their various demands known. As soon as they do, reason is resuscitated, for to say anything is to assert the law of identity. Without that law (viz., a thing is itself) their demand for Black Studies, for example, could be met by distributing green hats. If Black Studies are not Black Studies, they could be anything except Black Studies. In order to get a program in Black Studies they must say "We want Black Studies, not green hats. A equals A." It would be difficult, however, to imagine a besieged administrator wresting concessions on the laws of thought from radicals. Such effeteness would be ludicrous in a mob confrontation. Radicals thus have it both ways, presupposing that reason is valid by the act of speaking, but denying its validity when caught in a contradiction. Their mental processes continue but they use them to create non-thought which corresponds to what they "feel." Anti-rationalism, born of sloppy thinking, engenders even greater sloppy thinking.

To possess a set of beliefs which organize and explain the world is one of man's strongest desires. To find a credo that will withstand the cold winds of reason, one must be prepared to search hard and long. Once reason is gotten out of the way, however, belief comes easily. Armed with contempt for truth, for the law of non-contradiction, and for difficult enterprises, a person can take his desires for reality. He can accept the systems — Marxism, existentialism, and determinism — whose presuppositions underlie the radical's arguments on all issues, including violence. A simple and total explanation of the world is the most satisfying. The success of Marxism should thus not be surprising. Marx himself found it so simplistic that he declared, "I am not a Marxist." It has the extra advantage of including in its formulation two other extremely sloppy ideas:

Marxian dialectics presupposes relativism and purports to re-place reason. The application of Marxist theories to American life is an inevitable source of violence for two reasons. First, Marx recommends supporting "every revolutionary movement against the existing social and political order of things." (These words are quotes from the *Communist Manifesto*). Revolutionary movements are by definition violent. Second, Marxian dialectics is a source of fresh sloppy thinking.

One of the objections to Marxism which even Marxists under-stood was the argument from human nature. Man, it runs, is by nature competitive, territorial, and possessive. Therefore, a system built on co-operation, in which one works, not for per-sonal profit, but for the commonweal, cannot succeed: it is built on a lie. Existentialism, itself a simple, comprehensive, and completely gratuitous doctrine, seems tailor-made to answer these objections. Sartre, existentialism's vulgarizer, probably adopted the system for that very reason. According to the roadside existentialist, existence precedes essence. One only has an essence when dead ("You are what you become," etc.) One cannot, therefore, speak of "human nature": if there were such a thing, it would be an essence. In its place is put our "existential be-coming" (i.e., we exist). Through existentialism it becomes possible to make up a system for the government of man which in no way takes account of their nature. The essential factor is removed from the debate! Marxism becomes an acceptable theory.

Relativism, existentialism, anti-rationalism, and Marxism all act to destroy the analytical spirit. They were born in minds either devoid of clear ideas or uninterested in truth. Social science, the other prime force for illogic in our generation, does not, in theory, have much in common with relativism, Marxism, or anti-intellectualism. Psychology and sociology are referred to by their practitioners as "sciences." Careful analysis, impec-cable observation, and healthy skepticism are all implied by this term. Whereas relativism denies the concept of truth, sociology and psychology seek an objective and verifiable truth. Whereas irrationalists deny the law of non-contradiction, sociologists and psychologists consider contradiction to be a sure sign of error. And finally, whereas relativism and anti-rationalism commit many of their blunders in the name of morality, sociology and psychology are rigidly deterministic, thus amoral. Psychology, the more serious of the two disciplines (and therefore a better example) has as its goal the prediction of behavior. The psychologist maintains that if he knew all the hereditary and environmental factors involved, he could *predict* every single gesture, word, and thought of his subject. It follows that man's behavior is *totally* determined. If it were not, how could one possibly predict with perfect accuracy? We are therefore not responsible for our acts, gestures, and thoughts. Responsibility, by definition, implies choice. Choice, by definition, implies freedom. If we cannot help doing what we do, or thinking what we think, how can we be responsible? If you program a robot to kill, you don't say that it is evil when it carries out orders. It is a machine. Likewise, determined man is a machine. The terms good and bad are devoid of meaning for a consistent psychologist.

Yet among the radical professors preaching to students and intimidating unpoliticized professors, sociologists and psychologists are consistently the most numerous. One of the founders of SDS, supposedly a student organization, is in fact the professor of sociology Richard Flacks. When it comes to moral condemnation of our society and references to absolute justice, none are louder than these determinists. Here is non-thought at its most incredible. The moralizing psychologist contradicts the most basic tenet of his discipline. Either psychology is nonsense or he is speaking nonsense.

This sloppiness influences thousands of students each year, for sociology and psychology are well respected by the un-educated. Doubters are silenced by fears of being branded psychotic by the psychologists, who have special pejorative epithets in their jargon for those who are not utterly convinced of the validity of their discipline. Psychology and sociology are very easy subjects in colleges and students wanting good grades for little work, as well as those who wish to understand man, flock to courses in them. Those interested in social work take sociology courses thinking that they are for that purpose. So many students have done so and become professors in turn that there is now some truth to the idea.

The general public regards sociologists and psychologists as experts in the fields of race relations, child rearing, law, and government, all of which are closely related to radical agitation. Their pronouncements on moral questions are considered the *result* of their research rather than a contradiction of the basic assumption of that research. In an authoritarian world made possible by anti-rationalism and relativism, the social scientist is a respected authority.

How, one might ask, can the psychologists be so irrational as to contradict their most cherished belief with such regularity? I have already suggested that psychological problems often caused them to take up psychology in the first place. In addition, it must be mentioned that social sciences are a catch-all for those without any special aptitudes. Mathematics takes a unique talent without which one is lost after basic calculus. Physics and chemistry require a similar gift. Aptitude for languages is something one either has or does not have. The same can be said for literature. Biology requires lesser special aptitudes, as do history and area studies. It would be difficult to affirm, however, that any scholarly endeavor whatsoever requires less special talent than sociology or psychology. If you can read and write, you are qualified. It is thus the student who is either dull or sick who most often continues in the field.

This sociological analysis of the question should make many sociologists' attitudes more comprehensible. Their knowledge of their own inferiority makes them rabid egalitarians in all spheres. If everyone is equal, they reason, they are too. They are consequently the foremost proponents of letting students vote in matters of policy. They are invariably against breadth requirements. As non-linguists, non-mathematicians and writers whose reputation for jargon is notorious, they do not want the university sanctifying these skills with a requirement. As frauds, a cynic would say, it is in their interest to prevent students from becoming critical enough, through a good education, to see through them.

The fact that they are irrational enough to spout morality while believing that there is no such thing is not surprising when one considers that their entire discipline is founded on contradiction: if man is determined (a supposition abandoned by real science years ago), sociologists and psychologists are also determined. Therefore, when they say anything about man (e.g., that he is determined) they are merely making determined noises. One cannot say of a determined noise that it is *true*. To find the truth, man must have liberty. The idea of finding truth implies the possibility to see what *is*, to have a choice. Of course, what a machine says *may* be true. There is simply no way for another machine to know it. If, for example, there were men on Mars, we could say that *they* were determined and that we were speaking objective truth. We could refer to truth because we would be outside the determined order. If, on the other hand, we are inside a determined system, we are pawns whose utterances are not worthy of notice.

People are rational by nature. None can conceive of two opposite statements which are simultaneously true (contradiction). Yet, for reasons too numerous to discuss here, they make errors in reasoning. Nevertheless they cannot avoid sensing, however vaguely, the contradictions inherent in relativism, anti-rationalism, and the social sciences. The gift of reason makes life even more confusing for them. They accept the dogmas of the day but have a pinched and bewildered look. The contrast between the objections of reason and the dogma creates total befuddlement. The goal of a good education is to bring this latent rationality to the surface. The problem is that the student's chances of getting one are growing smaller and smaller.

The sociologists and psychologists bear the major responsibility for the direction of American elementary and secondary education. In its vulgarized version, Deweyism has eschewed work, discipline, and thought for "self-expression" and personality development. Its basic idea is that it matters little what the pupil says, provided that he "open up." Whatever he says must be greeted by cheers so that he will continue to express himself. Criticism is therefore practically eliminated. Under the influence of Piaget, Freud, and Froebel, the idea that the pupil works for reward (grades) has been replaced by the doubtful theory that children have a natural inclination for work.

It is well known that most activists come from upper middle-class families and that their parents have all read books on child-rearing written by psychologists or doctors versed in psychology. These parents are tolerant, liberal, enlightened, and anxious to do what is best for the child. They are relativistic enough to try anything and therefore blindly follow the authorities. The modern parent consequently reasons with the child instead of using authority. He is not supposed to order his progeny about. He must marshal convincing arguments. The child becomes the equal of his parent. He quickly learns arrogance and bad faith in order to win arguments and escape from all control. These are, strangely enough, the chief faults of the college radical.

When the child goes to school, he is placed in the hands of a semi-literate woman who has learned the Dewey gospel in education classes. No pupil must be made to feel inferior, however inferior he may be. In high school the general climate is the same. No one is ever mistaken, illogical, or foolish in liberal arts subjects. It is only in math and science that right and wrong cannot be eliminated (in our universities, radicals are rarely science or math majors). In innumerable discussions, the pupil has spoken up and gotten approval for expressing himself. His teachers believe, like his old schoolmarm, that all opinions are equal; the important thing is to express oneself and not be inhibited. It's been proven by social science. For the two or three papers the pupil has had to write in high school, he has gotten A or A plus unless his spelling was abysmal. Therefore, he reasons, he must be intelligent. His ideas, being those of an intelligent person, should be taken very seriously indeed.

This is an excellent recipe for producing a know-nothing monster. Salvation has traditionally come in America in two ways: the 70 per cent of college prep students relegated to inferior universities realized that they were not geniuses and adjusted to that fact. Most still do. Until the end of the fifties the 30 per cent of the graduates admitted to reasonably good universities came to realize their nullity in the very first semester.

They were graded and criticized for the first time. Their ideas were found foolish, unoriginal, self-contradictory, and gratuitous. They realized that they really had not yet analyzed anything. They were often quite miserable as they discovered the truth about themselves and the world. This was education, a very bitter but marvelously healthy pill to swallow. Few people really desire such enlightenment, for self-love is against it. It is only man's weakest passion—the love of truth—which pushes him into it. Students are not going to impose such a system on themselves. That is the professor's duty.

The fact that college students are less and less required to face their limitations can be partially explained by the increasingly lower faculty standards at American universities. The need for more professors has admitted a certain number of morons to faculties in better colleges. A professor incapable of criticizing students' ideas is worse than useless.

A number of changes in courses and curricula have equally contributed to the stifling of useful criticism. A student in the 1950's was usually obliged to take ten semester courses a year. The content of most of the courses taken in the first two years was fixed by requirements. The last two years were mostly spent in meeting requirements for the major. During his four years of college, the student was consequently exposed to forty professors, most of whom he had not been allowed to pick for their congeniality. How could he avoid some serious criticism and therefore a chance to improve the clarity and profundity of his thinking?

During the academic year, a student now typically takes only eight semester courses (in many places six) including such formerly unthinkable subjects as Tutoring in the Community (teaching children to read and write). About half the breadth requirements have been eliminated on the average, although this varies greatly from college to college. It is typical for a student to be exposed in four years to only twenty-eight professors, most of whom he can choose for their benevolence. Only in his major subject will he be seriously criticized. He can thus become a competent enough specialist without ever having his logic corrected in a good philosophy course, his organization of ideas criticized in a good history course, or his understanding of what lies under the surface of a poem examined in a literature course. As the perusal of any student newspaper shows, and his talk about the "irrelevance" of university curricula notwithstanding, he can easily graduate without learning to talk to any subject whatsoever.

Little changes in requirements, curricula, and admission standards can have a surprisingly great overall effect. Many graduates of respectable universities today are incredibly ignorant, are incapable of understanding an argument with more than one strand, or even of completing a simple sentence. Their ignorance causes them to take old ideas which have failed for creative innovations and new ideas which work for old failures. Their inability to reason leads to their fear of "sterile intellectualism" and their reliance on action. Their inability to complete a simple sentence leads to numerous repetitions of "you know" and "I mean" followed by nods of complicity which seem to say "If you agree with me, I'll agree with you." If we do not agree, we must expect trouble.

One link between the students who were to become radicals in the 1960's and their professors was general agreement on the verities of politics. They were both liberals. Here was more encouragement for the student to think himself equal to his professor. Had they not both reached the same conclusions on weighty matters by independent reflection? The war in Vietnam was not only a crucial moment in United States history, but a turning point in the development of campus violence. The professors at first played an honorable role. They pointed out—with reasoned discourse and a sense of fair play—the weaknesses of American Far East policy. They became the nation's conscience. As early as 1965, however, professorial petitions took on a self-important and self-righteous tone. The professors seemed no more interested in truth than General Westmoreland's public relations men. In March, 1965, for example, a group of respected Yale professors—John Blum, Karl Deutsch, Gene Mostow, Robert Triffin, Mary Wright, and Robert Dahl—en-

dorsed and sent to the President a letter advising negotiations to
end the war. It made five points, three of which were irrelevant.
Its two main arguments contradicted each other. On the one
hand, it claimed that bombing North Vietnam would be absurd,
because the struggle in South Vietnam was a civil war. On the
other, it affirmed that the war could be settled only by the leaders of the Soviet Union and Communist China. (A civil war, it
should be remembered, is one among citizens, or parties, of a
single state.) Nevertheless, three of the signers explained to re-
porters that the letter's value consisted in its "tight reasoning."
Indeed, other letters, petitions, and speeches were much worse.
Appeal was no longer being made to reason, but to the pleasures
of moral indignation.

If the professors—professional intellectuals—thought other
goals, such as peace, more important than truth, why should
the students seriously examine the issues? They re-created the
doctrine of individual nullification, used by the southern states in
order to keep their slaves.

No law was to be obeyed which did not meet with the
approval of the students' consciences. The law that everyone
had in mind was, of course, the draft for Vietnam. The professors, sharing the students' distaste for the war, refrained
from refuting them on the issue of individual nullification. This
was surely a mistake, for those who follow their consciences
without having reflected on the problems of conscience end up
following the most charismatic speakers and writers. Those
Germans mesmerized by Hitler, for example, were following
their consciences. They despised reason and intellectual debate.
They considered an emotional appeal morally superior to dry
argumentation. Hitler himself was following his conscience in
exterminating millions.

Yet somehow the radical professors, with the tacit assent of
the moderate timid professors, put Hitler in the camp of those
who wanted the law obeyed. Comparisons between the concentration camps of the Third Reich and the American Selective Service System were bandied about by radical professors
without forceful refutation by moderates. The radicals argued
that Hitlerian officers who had wantonly killed millions were
judged guilty at the Nuremberg trials even though they had

obeyed orders. An American could therefore refuse induction if it was against his conscience. The lesson of Nuremberg would, in fact, be that a government which grants no civil liberties, right of opposition, elections, or procedures for change can carry out the dictates of the conscience of one man, the ruler, and that a single conscience is often a very bad guide indeed. To disobey one man's orders (e.g., Hitler's) is to value one's own conscience more than that one man's. To disobey laws maintained despite a free press, review by an independent judiciary, and frequent elections is quite a different matter. It is to claim infallibility and refuse equality before the law. Only a master race would have the right to do so.

If one admits a right of disobedience to the law, no law need ever be obeyed. The very term law becomes meaningless: a law which is not binding is nothing more than advice. If law is destroyed, what can replace it but the rule of force? To disobey the law in a democracy is therefore inevitably worse than disobeying one's conscience, for it would lead, if practiced by all, to the obligation to obey hundreds of *illegitimate* orders made by the totalitarian force which would replace the rule of law. This argument does not, of course, apply to the test case, in which a law is disobeyed in order that its constitutionality may be judged. Such "disobedience" is based on doubts over what the law is and seeks a definitive ruling which will end confusion. It consequently strengthens the rule of law.

Perhaps there are some reasonable arguments in favor of civil disobedience in a democracy. I have never heard one, however, for the professors made no effort to marshal them. The radicals contented themselves with irrational and demagogic sloganeering while the moderates remained silent. The intellectuals had become anti-intellectuals.

How could one expect students to react? The character of protest began to change. Moral indignation pushed students into violent acts against the violence of the war. The destruction of reason prevented them from seeing the contradiction.

The same sloppy doctrine of individual nullification contributed to violence related to civil rights. Professors and students had had an excellent influence as long as they had remained on the side of law. In the fifties, the Southerners were outlaws refusing to integrate as required by law because they felt they should follow *their* consciences! At that time it was obvious to the professors that individual nullification was evil. When, however, they refused to speak out against the doctrine of civil disobedience used to obtain advantages for blacks, the shoe was on the other foot. When Negro leaders began to say that the law was stacked against blacks, very few professors mentioned that American law is the best friend any member of any minority group has. The visceral approach was accepted and the symbol of the law became, not the Supreme Court or the Bill of Rights, but the policeman with sunglasses and a club. In order to be in favor of civil rights, it became necessary to approve—at the very least, to "understand"—black segregationists.

Few eminent professors spoke out sharply against Black Power groups. Criticism was muted by the desire to show that one realized that white racism was really to blame. This silence was tacit permission for racial hatred and its inevitable companion, violence.

Slipshod thinking has thus been enshrined. It is equated with purity in the minds of the radicals. Relativism ushered in irrationalism, which makes a joke of free inquiry and the search for truth. The university, an institution devoted to rational discourse and the search for truth, is, consequently, an absurdity. Marxism, dependent on relativism and dialectics, is a systematic theory for the destruction of clear thought. Determinism destroys the very notion of truth, for the term is meaningless in a determined world. Sociology and psychology spawn theories preventing education from taking place.

Relativism, anti-rationalism, Marxism, sociology, and psychology make of their disciples permanent sloppy thinkers. Once a person has drowned his rationality in order to become a follower of Marx or Skinner, he has made a permanent decision to stifle the objections reason proposes. Reason soon raises fewer and fewer of them until the disciple is a brainwashed creature incapable of handling anything intelligently. The radical student is the perfect example. He treats every new question which arises with the slovenly thinking habits fostered by the self-contradictory ideas he has already accepted.

The result can be seen in the following example taken from the *Davis Enterprise*. Two leaders of radical student groups explain why they are picketing military recruiters at the Davis campus of the University of California:

"In Lee's [the leader of Resistance] view society is basically divided into two classes: the ruling class as exemplified in the regents and the industrialist interests and the people, composed of students and working class members who must fight the war. The upper class protects its interests by training students at the university to become managers who manipulate the working class unable to attend college, he said.

" 'You are all the proud owners of a 2-S deferment—you can participate in the war in any way you want. They have given you a deal, but what are you going to do when they offer you the next deal?'

"The essence of the system, continued Lee, is exploitation of authority—third world people [sic]. He challenged students to reject the capitalistic offer to share in this oppression. The Resistance speaker told students that military recruiters had no business on a university campus. 'Some people say that this is depriving others of the right of free speech, but the military deprives people of the right of free speech and life.'

"Saying that American corporate interests overseas would go as far as killing to make a profit, Lee declared: 'The military recruiters have no right on campus. It is our duty and responsibility to kick them off.' He also informed students, 'The war is at home, I hope I don't end up fighting you people on the streets.'

"SDS member Rusty Staub followed Lee and focused on the imperialist character of American capitalism. He said that the economic system could sustain itself only if employers pay employees a lower wage than the value of the product produced [sic] and by extending itself throughout the world.

"As evidence of this contention, Staub pointed to the economic interests the United States has in Vietnam. 'The United States needs Vietnam. We're fighting communism there on economic rather than moral grounds,' he said. According to the speaker, the vast tin deposits in Bolivia are becoming more inaccessible to this country because of reaction from third world peoples, making the Vietnam deposits all the more crucial."

2

ISSUES

Issues Not Directly Related to the University

The causes discussed in the preceding chapter produce hatred
but do not produce violence directly. A man does not strike another because he hates him. He must first find a justification. In
radical politics this is called resolving an issue. It is by applying muddled thinking and false suppositions to political issues
that the radical rouses himself to the pitch of violence.

The idea prevalent in society is that the radical positions on
the issues, although extreme, have a great deal of merit.
Naturally no group is ever completely wrong on everything.
McCarthyism, for example, was legitimately concerned with
foreign espionage in the United States. It was nevertheless a
basically repressive movement destined to terrorize unfortunates
who had sincerely believed that communism was a new human-
ism. Had it not been checked by the workings of a democratic
system, civil liberties would eventually have been threatened.
McCarthy's solution was plainly worse than the problem. Hitler,
too, was occasionally right. It would be difficult to dispute his
assertion that the class structure in Germany was too rigid. It
was practically impossible for a talented German youth from a
working-class family to become a doctor, lawyer, or university
professor. The *Führer's* solution was nevertheless plainly worse
than the problem.

In like fashion, radical students have dug up a few legitimate
causes of concern. It is true that there are more racism, materialism, and depersonalization in America than most of us
would like to see here. Unfortunately, radical solutions, if put
into effect, would actually increase these ills. They would also,
like the solutions of Joseph McCarthy and Adolf Hitler, lead

us to totalitarian government. That is, in any case, what this essay attempts to prove.

The basic accusation and major issue of the radical is the corruption of our institutions. They are evil because they produce racism, materialism, wars of imperialism, exploitation of workers and "Third-World people," rule by an elite insensitive to the needs of human beings, pollution, and a melting pot where groups lose their own culture. Unlike radicals of the thirties who compared our miserable existence to idyllic life in Russia, today's radicals use no culture, past or present, as a point of comparison. When asked to what they are comparing American institutions, radicals have no answer. It is to their dreams that they are comparing them. Here we see an obvious contradiction, for they insist on the one hand that if the United States is not perfect, it is perfectly corrupt (which of course does not follow) while demanding no such perfection of themselves. This contradiction is easily explained by their upbringing and is justified by the sociologist's doctrine that the individual is never at fault. How can a determined product of heredity and environment be guilty? All evil is the fault of society. It is therefore society rather than oneself which should change. As I have mentioned, however, the radical cannot adopt this position without contradicting himself: in a determined world, society is just as blameless as the individual. The very idea of changing society, moreover, implies the liberty to act otherwise than destiny would wish.

It is in this first contradictory assertion that radicals ground their rhetoric. One cannot penetrate radical "thought" without understanding that it applies relative—and extremely lenient—moral standards to radicals, but absolute—and intransigent—ones to society (the "system").

Radicals generally couch their complaints in Marxist terms. It is fair to say that if the New Left does not want communism, it has nevertheless swallowed whole the Marxist critique of capitalism. This explains the amusing references to the exploited workers, supposed allies of the students in the revolution. There is of course no group less revolutionary (or less exploited) than American workers, but when you accept a dogma you cannot make an exception of its fundamental thesis.

The Marxist interpretation of history is exclusively materialistic, which in work-a-day language means that Marxists in-
terpret everything in economic terms. Metaphysical materialism has only the most tenuous links to economic materialism.
Thus the ridiculous assertion by the SDS leader quoted in the
preceding chapter that the United States is fighting in Vietnam for control of that country's gigantic tin deposits! The
fact that there are no tin mines (He uses the term "deposits"
for both Bolivia and Vietnam, implying that the situation is
the same in both countries. This is of course false since in
Bolivia there are tin mines.) in Vietnam does not stop a
Marxist critic, who must find an economic explanation for
everything or change credos. Neither does the fact that any
country with tin is only too happy to sell it and therefore does
not need to be "conquered." The Marxist critic disdainfully
ignores such embarrassing phenomena as the rise in the capitalists' stock market whenever peace is rumored and its fall whenever the war escalates.

Although economics is the alpha and omega of the Marxian
universe, the radical reproaches American society for excessive
"materialism," by which he means interest in G.N.P., goods,
and property. One of the characters in a radical fable read over
a New Left radio station (KPFA) in 1968 was an evil swine
who enslaved people. His name was Gross Nasty Pig. In radical
rhetoric the American system is monstrous because it incarnates
the implacable quest for economic growth at any cost. As
Marxist interpreters, however, radicals should approve. Making
the economy strong and the people comfortable are so important to Marxists that in all countries where they reign, man's
basic freedoms have been sacrificed to these goals. If radicals
thought clearly enough to realize this contradiction, they would
also understand that the American system is really to a great
extent the absence of an imposed system. It is possible to say
of a free society that it contains materialistic people, but not
that the structure itself is materialistic. American law contains
no injunction to create wealth. It simply allows people to do as
they please. The radical's idea of the individual's innocence
and society's guilt again leads him into error.

Racism is one of the most serious charges levelled against America. This is because it is true. The Marxist explanation is that capitalism causes racism. The radicals agree, for man is good and racism is bad. It must therefore be attributed to the "system." If they were not illogical, they would seriously seek out empirical justification for their thesis by investigating racism in "socialist" or "people's" republics. These countries do not consider themselves worthy of the name "communist," but they have been on the road towards communism for many years now, and one would expect some result. The most cursory investigation of the U.S.S.R. reveals, however, that the Chechen, Ingush, Karachai, Balkar, Kalmyk, Crimean Tartars, and Jews are the victims of far greater racism than any known in the United States. Indeed, it is government-sponsored racism, the most pernicious, because it leads to pogroms and concentration camps. There have even been incidents in Moscow created by people resentful of the presence in universities of a mere handful of Africans (these, of course, were not encouraged by the government). Either the radicals have not looked into this or, worse, they *have* done so, and have decided to remain silent about what they have seen.

The mystical and unmaterialistic Orient would provide equally fertile ground for comparison studies. Here we find feared and despised Chinese minorities in several countries, such as Thailand and Indonesia. The persecution of Hindus in Pakistan and of Moslems in India is well known. In Africa, Nigerians despise Biafrans because they are short and ambitious. In South Africa, it is not only whites and Negroes who fail to live in harmony. Indians and Negroes live in mutual suspicion which occasionally explodes into violence. In Latin America, Indians and mestizos regard each other as less than human.

We should not, one might object, compare ourselves to these underdeveloped peoples, but to the civilized population of Europe. The objection is not only racist but badly taken. Slovaks hate Hungarians. Poles hate Germans and Russians. Finns hate Swedes and Russians. Czechs and Slovaks hate each other, as do the Flemish and Walloons. The Serbs, Croats, and Slovenes despise one another. The Irish hate the English, and the English despise the Irish. The Irish of County Cork hate the Irish of County Connaught. The French are not overly fond of Algerians, nor the Swiss of "Latins." The Germans are not without their racial distastes. Darker Italians from the south are treated as inferiors by northern Italians.

Indeed, these webs of hatred have led to genocide, committed not only by Germans but by the British in Tasmania, the Dutch in South Africa, the Portuguese in Brazil, and the Russians in Hungary and in the Soviet Union.

Far from being an American invention, as radicals claim, racism is so common that in Brewton Berry's *Race and Ethnic Relations* (1958), racial harmony is treated as a special exception. In the three cases cited by Berry (pp. 115-121), unusual factors apparently play a large part in causing it. In the case of the Tungus and the Cossacks of Manchuria, for example, the cause of harmony seems to be their shared hatred for a third race, their Chinese neighbors!

A fair look at the world would show that the United States, although far from perfect, is one of the least racist countries in the world. Our civil rights laws go further and have more teeth than those of any other country. Those against discrimination in jobs and housing are practically unique. Britain is usually considered by Americans to be free of racism. Yet Brian MacArthur of the London *Times* (hardly a pro-American newspaper) admits that "one often wishes that the same sincere commitment to equal job opportunities for minority groups that exists in America could be detected in Britain" (February 8, 1969). If Black Power and violence had not come upon the scene, aided by radicals, racism would have continued to decrease. It would not have disappeared, however, because it is human nature to mistrust people who are different from oneself, no matter how small the difference. In Alsace, for example, there are two large towns whose inhabitants, of the same ethnic stock, speak practically the same dialect. Nevertheless the residents of Strasbourg look upon the residents of Mulhouse as a mentally inferior group, whereas the latter accuse the former of being a cold, snobbish people.

The ways to mitigate racism are well known: (1) Cause people of different races to come into equal-status contact, and (2) educate them. The civil rights laws are taking care of equal-status contact. Education should now be the primary goal of anti-racists. Radicals, however, wish, by their own admission, to destroy the educational system. They also encourage blacks to segregate into Black Power groups, thus eliminating the beneficial effects of civil rights laws. Their stands seem designed, not to combat this cancer in American society, but to nurture it. One is consequently tempted to conclude that the accusation that America is a racist society is, for radicals, an excuse to "change the institutions," not a vital interest in itself.

This is corroborated by the fact that they have created their own racism every bit as vicious as the original version. Racism has little to do with races or sub-races. Jews, for example, are neither zoologically nor anthropologically a race. Neither are Germans. Yet the hatred of Jews or Germans is widely recognized as racism. The essence of racism is the division of humanity by race, nationality, language, culture, profession, or any other standard, into groups, some of which are branded "evil" or "inferior" and others "moral" or "superior." Thus SDS divides society into evil exploiters with filthy-pig henchmen ("the lackeys of imperialism") and the "people" (SDS supporters).

This radical version of racism is doubly foolish: first, it condemns racism while being racist. Second, it contradicts the radical claim that not man, but society is evil. There should be no "pigs" in the world if man is good. Our radical could object that the evil society is nevertheless at fault: evil societies inevitably produce pigs. In that case, however, how does he explain his own purity?

Radicals have introduced a second type of racism, that of age. The young are good and the old corrupt. Slaveowners used the idea that Negroes were inferior to keep their economic system going. Anyone who objected was called a "Nigger-lover." So radicals use solidarity based on age to gain converts, implying that to be non-radical is to be a traitor to one's age group.

The radical is not only wrong on the issue of racism in relation to capitalism but dangerously wrong. For if there are still some Americans who think that whites are superior to blacks or vice versa, very few speak of *punishing* or *suppressing* the inferiors. Herbert Marcuse, the most beloved saint of student radicalism, has, on the other hand, implied that "pigs" be silenced by any means necessary. His followers obviously agree.

The war in Vietnam is the other important radical "proof" that the United States is corrupt. Certainly anyone of good faith must admit that an excellent case for American withdrawal from Vietnam exists. He must also admit, however, that reasonably good cases can be made for escalation, the status quo, and limited withdrawal. It is equally obvious that each alternative has its problems. The radical case is not a strategic one or even a tactical one in which the interests of the United States play a role. Neither does it take into account international law, which sanctions aiding governments in power but condemns propping up revolutionary groups. It is a purely "moral" argument based on the fact that in Vietnam there is killing. Killing is evil. Therefore the United States is immoral. This approach is defensible, but its consequence is that no violence—for all violence eventually leads to killing—is permissible under any circumstances. Why then are student radicals violent? Why then do they condone Viet Cong atrocities? Why do they support the killing of "pigs"? Violence cannot be simultaneously unthinkable under any circumstances (in Vietnam) and legitimate in certain circumstances (ushering in the millenium).

To their basic contradictory position, they add two reasonable, morally-based arguments taken from non-radical critics of the war. The first is that the North Vietnamese government has the support of the South Vietnamese people. If true, it would be sufficient cause for American withdrawal from Vietnam. The problem, for a person who seeks the truth, is that no proof has been presented either for or against this allegation. The second is that civilians are being killed in Vietnam. This perfectly revolting fact applies, however, to almost all modern wars. The firebombing of German cities and the atomic bombing of Japanese cities were no less bloody. The argument should thus be directed against all wars and all participants in them.

These non-radical arguments are respectable, but not so incontrovertible as to legitimize an orgy of moral indignation.

To them, radicals add a number of absurdities. They accuse the United States of racism because the Viet Cong and North Vietnamese are Orientals. Are the South Vietnamese to be accused of hatred for Orientals as well? The radicals underline the horrors of napalm, as if bullets and poisoned spikes were somehow morally superior. They suggest that the United States is defending its economic interests in Vietnam when it has none. They affirm that the capitalists wage war to keep the economy going, when businessmen are practically unanimous in blaming the war for all the present economic woes.

The radicals are wrong on Vietnam, not only because their analysis is gratuitous and simplistic, but also because they are violent in the cause of peace and because they claim the right to obey their consciences rather than the law. As mentioned at the end of the preceding chapter, they bring in Nuremberg to defend themselves. When the law punishes their draft-dodging, they cry out that the police state has come to America. But are they ready to allow Southerners the right to refuse civil rights to Negroes because they know in their hearts that God wanted colored folks to chop cotton without pay? If not, they are either sloppy thinkers, totalitarians or both.

"Depersonalization" is a word used by radicals to depict the feeling people often have that events are beyond them, that real human contact is becoming less and less a part of everyday life. As in the case of racism, the basic accusation is not without merit. Their thesis that the "American system" is to blame, however, is another matter. Their solution—that we should follow their example—is ridiculous. As with racism, the radical solution is worse than the problem. The tribal organization of radical groups is much less personal and individualistic than that of the rest of American society. There is nothing, by definition, more impersonal than a mob without reason.

To the extent—quite large—that their complaints take on a Luddite ("smash the computer") ring, radicals are in direct contradiction with their desire to see workers, blacks, and "Third-World peoples" live decently. What could be more dehumanizing than a life of drudgery in which one does by hand

and foot what can be done by machine, thanks to the brain? The radicals' upper middle-class background, combined as always with sloppy thinking, has left them unable to imagine what pre-industrial society was like. While railing at shocking poverty in the United States among blacks, they forget that our highly mechanized industry and agriculture have made the median income of blacks in the United States higher than that of whites in any of the Common Market countries. The New Left radio fable mentioned before features a bear revolting against the bourgeois world of work. Why should one want to own those filthy and useless objects which Gross Nasty Pig hungers after, he asks. When he invites his girl friend to dinner, however, this enemy of consumerism opens his refrigerator (frostless no doubt) and takes out all sorts of gourmet foods. For the radical student, this fable is quite realistic. He has been talking like that bear and living like that bear for twenty, sometimes thirty years. He is no more aware than that hirsute omnivore of the fact that only a highly mechanized society can allow people like him, who produce nothing—or even those who work—to consume products and services with such gluttony.

The depersonalization argument is, at its best, the anguished cry that despite liberty and abundance, man is not happy; or more specifically that the protestor is not happy. It is easy to see from the preceding how he reasons: man is good. Therefore he deserves to be happy. He is not. Society must somehow be responsible and is therefore corrupt.

It is often said that radicals are idealistic, meaning that they have high standards. In this example, the generalization holds true. The radical's standards for what he is "entitled to," for what he "has coming" are very high indeed. He simply cannot see why government should not give him happycare.

Very often the issue has a more specific meaning. What the radical (along with many others) misses is a feeling of community, of belonging to a group. This tribal instinct was perfectly satisfied, as one would expect, in the tribe, where it shared the stage with conformism, ignorance, intolerance, injustice, slavery, poverty, and disease. It was partially satisfied in the small towns and small colleges where one was *of* the community whether one liked it or not. Industrialization, specialization, and big state and federal governments have all done their bit in destroying the tight-knit community.

The New Left and hippy movements can certainly be seen as moves back towards tribalism. Having formed their tribes, radicals have no ground for complaint on this issue any longer. Their problem is, of course, that if they stop complaining, the pretext for their tribe disappears.

Their mistake is in blaming "capitalism" or "U.S. imperialism." Depersonalization is much greater in statist societies, as the slightest contact with the works of Kafka or Solzhenitsyn shows. In the brave new world recommended by the radicals' guide (Marcuse), a Soviet-type spy system would be set up wherein anything subversive said to a neighbor would be reported to the local "People's Committee." It is difficult to see how this would bring about a genuine feeling of community. The "American system," on the other hand, allows people to form tribes if they so wish.

Neither is it wise to conclude that whatever gives community feeling is good. There are other values besides the tribe. War has traditionally given man the feeling of melting into a group greater than himself. Through it, he has experienced love and community (the confessions of Antoine in Martin du Gard's *The Thibaults* should make this clear to anyone unconvinced). Is the radical willing to praise war on this account? What then will become of his arguments for peace at any price? In fact, the radical who commits violence *is* getting the tribal satisfactions of the warrior. Since he is violent in the name of peace, however, he also gets the gratifications of the self-righteous pacifist. He has it both ways because his slovenly thinking never points out to him the incompatibility of these two joys.

While supposing that humanity is divided into two races, the "pigs" and the "people," radical students nevertheless maintain that everyone is equal. Therefore everyone should have equal deserts. Yet in America there is poverty and there is wealth. The system must be evil. This contradicts not only the radical's racism, but his theory that material goods are not really important.

The assumption of equality is of course false. Any policy based on it can therefore only lead to harm. Many experiments in community living have been made where all were treated equally in every way. Despite the fact that only those who wished to join did so, no community of this sort has survived long *with the same members*. In a society of mandatory equal compensation, the result would surely be worse. Such a society is in fact inconceivable, for those who enforced equality would be much more than the equals of those forced to submit to it. The Marxist habit of counting, not prestige and power, but money alone has blinded radicals to this obvious defect in their "just society."

An important corollary of the "man is good" theory is that the institution of property played a large part in corrupting society. The institution of property is evil. During the now infamous rioting over "People's Park" in Berkeley, the radicals got a chance to try out their theories on the subject. A vacant lot belonging to the University of California was adopted by "street people" (a low form of the hippy which inhabits the peripheries of large universities). As these people reject the work ethic and are consequently poor, they need free entertainments. Like the Roman masses under Domitian who chanted "bread and circuses," they are always ready for a little agitation. They had planted flowers and bushes on the lot and baptized it—at the suggestion of a crafty radical—"People's Park." The university, thinking things were getting out of hand, evicted the street people and erected a fence. Radicals decided to "liberate" (take over by force) what was now *their* property.

Local police could not restrain the mob. The National Guard was called in. Eventually there was a death and the radicals had the martyr they wanted. Here was proof of our society's corruption: it valued "property more than people." A law student writing in the *Davis Enterprise* opined that "the taking of one human life and the wounding of many others can hardly be justified in defense of property. Only the erratic even in the face of provocation would react so drastically." A group of Davis *professors* composed a position paper stating that "while it is true that the park legally belongs to the University, the issues are much larger than property rights. On the Davis campus we believe that *people's* rights are more important than property rights."

This sloganeering brings up the question of who are the "people." In the American system it is everybody, whence the doctrine of one man, one vote. Nobody speaks for the people. They express themselves by ballot. In this instance, the people had elected the governors who, over a period of years, had named the Regents of the University of California. These Regents, named under a system approved by the people, and which could be changed by ballot if the people so desired, are ultimately responsible for the appointment of faculty and general planning—including the use of University property. The people of California own the University and all its property. Consequently, the "People's Park" was a true people's vacant lot until it was taken over by a small self-appointed group calling itself the people. The radical idea that a small group understands the public's needs better than that public itself comes from Marx. For him, the communists were those who knew what the proletariat really wanted. Behind Marx stands Rousseau, whose "general will" was the infallible interpretation by the happy few of the real needs and desires of all. Such thinking is popular among the rulers of communist countries. It is their explanation for not letting the people vote (with a choice among candidates). Their chiefs know better what they want than they. General de Gaulle used the concept when he compared the grandeur of the "real" France, of which he was the prophet, to the petty desires of most Frenchmen, whom he called "calves." Kenneth Rexroth, a radical poet and essayist enamored of the "people," refers to the general public as "the millions of kinks that freak out in front of the boob tube . . ." (*El Gaucho*, May 28, 1969).

Thus in Marxist revolutions a small group seizes some piece of property and baptizes it the "people's." Without a knowledge of this peculiar definition, it is impossible to understand the use, in America, of such radical slogans as "Power to the people." Radical conduct in the "People's Park" rioting was based on the same definition. Radicals glorified the "people" in order to steal from the real people! They vilified the principle of property in order to get a piece of property.

That people would be hurt was obvious, for in a country of law, the law must be enforced. That this did not deter them is the proof that property was more important to them than people—even their own "people." Their use of the slogan "People are more important than property" must therefore be considered as either hypocritical or singularly cretinous. The slogan itself, moreover, is perfect nonsense: property laws, by definition, fit into the larger category of law. The real question is therefore whether people are more important than law. Such a question presupposes a conflict whereas, in fact, the people have freely chosen the rule of law precisely because it *helps* and *protects* them. If the people wished to change—or eliminate—property laws, they could do so. Indeed they could strike all laws from the books. There is legislative machinery in America for adding or removing laws by vote at any time.

The "People's Park" incident illustrates why people have made property laws. Without them there would be no way of deciding who may and who may not remain at a given place. Because of humankind's unfortunate tendency to seize things and say, "This is mine" (a radical says, "This is the people's," but he means the same thing) property laws are necessary. Without them, we would have the law of the jungle: the strongest and least scrupulous would take over. Such is the system radicals seek with slogans like "People are more important than property," and "Power to the people."

The other issues are even less worthy of the serious attention they have received. "Police brutality" is simply the cry of the spoiled child who is, for the first time, not accorded special privileges. Egalitarian in theory, the radical is nevertheless offended when the law is applied to him. Indeed the "issue" is so ridiculous that many radicals cannot help smiling when talking about it. For them, the cry "police brutality" is simply the easiest way to gain the sympathies of those people who have put mind below heart and have consequently become childishly easy to manipulate. The radical is much too brutal for him to complain of brutality. He is in favor of violence, but only on the condition that it be against the law rather than in its name. The fact that policemen can occasionally be provoked by experts in provocation is unfortunate but certainly to be expected. If humanity were so perfect that all policemen were unprovokable, no police would be needed.

To put the whole question of "repression" and "police brutality" into perspective, let us summarize the official policy for controlling riots, not in the U.S.S.R., or China, or even France, but in Great Britain, the country which is usually considered the least violent in the world and, with the United States, the least repressive. In the British Army course on "Duties in Aid of the Civil Power," the measures prescribed for a riot are as follows: once the Riot Act has been read, and written authority obtained from the civil power by the military commander, the order is given to shoot one man in the mob, the ringleader if he can be isolated, and to shoot *to kill*. The English realize that rule by law does not permit disobedience to the law. Once a single exception is made, there is no law but only influence and power.

Many radicals actually affirm that there is no freedom in America because one is obliged to obey the law! It is of course just the other way around. Law guarantees essential freedoms (the Bill of Rights) and prevents other individuals from taking them away (penal code). The radical idea of freedom, the right to do anything at all, could exist for only one person, who would, like Camus's Caligula, be master and tyrant of the world. Since he would have the right to take away their liberty, they would be slaves.

Radicals also declare that America is not free because it is not ruled by the *people*. If by the "people" (as in, "People are more important than property.") they mean themselves, their accusation is of course true. If they mean the general public, it is false: free elections are held with perfect regularity. The radical position, however, is that elections are meaningless because the press, television, and radio (the "mass media") are controlled by an evil clique of capitalist oppressors who prevent radical views from being expressed. At least this is what they say on radio, on television, and in the press every day.

If the radicals were in power, they would prevent non-radical views from being expressed. Marcuse has spelled out his system of repression in his *Repressive Tolerance*. Radical students have refused free speech to non-radicals all over the nation. They know, however, that they are morally superior to the capitalists and therefore assume that what they do which is despicable must automatically be done by the capitalists as well. The empirically verifiable fact of free speech in America is beyond their comprehension. Therefore they deny it.

Issues Related to the University

The basic assumption of radicals concerning education is that no "real" or "meaningful" education can take place until the institutions of society are changed. The university is a device used by the capitalists to brainwash the people. Academic freedom is bourgeois nonsense, neither possible nor desirable.

Logically then, radicals should not be in the university. Why waste four years being brainwashed? There are of course practical reasons, and radicals mention them when pinned down: draft avoidance and career opportunities. Both are poor excuses, however, for if one is to act out of expediency, what right has one to argue on moral grounds? The radical here applies his revolting distinction between mandatory absolute morality for others and relative or no morality for him. He violently rejects the democratic concept of one standard for all.

Even on the basis of expediency, his reasons for remaining in the university are unsatisfactory. With his low opinion of American society, can he find happiness getting a good job and being a "tool of the capitalists"? After what he has said about conscience's supremacy over law, does he really think he can live with himself on a 2-S (student) draft deferment?

If the Viet Cong are being oppressed and he recognizes no law but his conscience, why is he not fighting by their side? Unlike the radical of the thirties, who fought in Spain, he is not risking his life for his putative beliefs. Unlike pacifists of other times and places, he is not refusing to be violent in his advocacy of non-violence.

"Radical student" is really a contradiction in terms. Such a person's ideas on the world contradict his presence in an American university. The contradiction is even more profound than it seems, for even with different ideas on the issues, the radical's unquestioning and fanatical tenacity of belief makes it impossible for him to justify his presence in any university devoted to the pursuit of truth. For what is a student but a person who admits he is ignorant? What is a professor but one who claims knowledge and intelligence in some matter or other? If an individual is already capable of thinking clearly on all subjects and knows all the answers, he is very well educated indeed. He is not, in the true sense of the term, a student.

He could justify his presence in the university by stating that he is masquerading as a student in order to destroy from the inside a hated American institution. He wishes to remove the instrument which teaches people to distinguish between what is probable and what is improbable, between what is true and what is false. There is little chance of his speaking in this vein, however. To do so would imply that one must be incapable of thinking clearly to be a radical.

Although the radical student does, in fact, explain his presence at the university by the necessity to destroy it, he claims that it must be annihilated for another reason. The university is the training ground for the cadres, scientists, engineers, and propagandists without whom the capitalists could no longer play their evil game. Transposed into non-conspiratorial terms, the idea is true: a modern democracy cannot survive without a reasonably literate electorate and a good number of well-trained, rational, and fair-minded people in positions of importance. The university now trains half the general public and almost all of those people destined by their merit to be the future leaders of the republic. Its destruction is therefore a logical step towards uprooting the system.

If one keeps the avowed radical goal of destruction in mind, the issues radicals create are no longer surprising. What more could one do to destroy education than to propose the elimination of requirements, grades, competitive admissions, and work? These radical demands can be summed up under the generic heading "self-determination for students." The rationale (for the consumption of those who do not want the university destroyed) is that students know their "needs" better than anyone else and should therefore decide all questions pertaining to students. Followed to its logical end, it would create a university in which students had complete control and the faculty obeyed orders. One wonders what sort of professor would work under such a system.

The principal defect in this rationale is that if students are masters, they are, by definition, no longer students. What they really need is not necessarily what they think they need (just as what hospital patients think they need is not necessarily what they really need). How could they reach an educated opinion of their "needs" when they are not yet educated? If people who have not yet graduated from a university are as capable of running one as those who have, does this not mean that the graduates gained nothing at all by attending a university? In that case, education, being worthless, might as well be eliminated altogether. The radical rationale, ostensibly concerned with improving education, implies that it is valuable (i.e., worth improving). The argument is therefore contradictory.

One might, of course, object that, according to my line of reasoning, those who have not attended college would be equally incapable of knowing their needs. Some undemocratic principle could then be deduced. Nothing is further from the truth. Those who have never attended college would certainly need guidance on their *educational* needs. This in no way implies that they need political guidance. On the contrary, the common man in the United States votes, not on the basis of half-understood abstractions about ideal political systems, but according to his interest. And this he understands perfectly well. The basis of democracy, one should remember, is the assumption that politics is not too complicated for the reasonably literate man. Radical students, on the other hand, have intellectual pretensions and would vote—if they believed in democracy—on the basis of abstract ideas which they understand no better than the common man.

There is another radical justification for giving students decision-making power in the university. It is that conception of equality which led to so much bloodshed in the French Revolution. We are all equal, not before God or before the law, but in every way. This of course contradicts the preceding rationale for self-determination, in which students were *more* qualified to judge their "needs" than anyone else. Nevertheless, radicals apply the theory with seeming logic: since we are all equal, each student, maintenance employee, faculty member, and administrator should have one vote. One man, one vote. Otherwise, the university is undemocratic. Here again, however, they contradict themselves, for they condemn the United States, with its principle of one man, one vote as undemocratic. Although some radicals voted for Eldridge Cleaver in the 1968 presidential campaign, most follow Marcuse in proclaiming that elections are a capitalistic trick.

To insist that the university be patterned after a hated government is the height of foolishness. The radicals' underlying assumption that a university should be run like a government is equally without merit. A university is no more a government than is an industrial firm, a newspaper, or an army. Government has as its business the settling of disputes, the preservation of rights and, to a certain extent, the commonweal. The university is concerned with the acquisition and distribution of truth. The decisions of national government affect everyone, for no one is allowed to disobey the law. University rules affect only those who have freely chosen to belong to the university community. American democracy posits that political wisdom is nobody's private property and that we are all equally fallible. It follows that an elite will govern no better than the representatives of the people. The university, on the contrary, claims professional superiority for its instructors. It is supposed that students will profit by coming into contact with their professors precisely because of this superiority.

The relationship between student and professor is, of course, like that between patient and doctor, or client and lawyer. On the one hand is the amateur, and on the other the professional. Indeed, what plumber or electrician would take suggestions from the customer on how to make a repair? Only the professor is timid enough even to entertain such an idea. The student's role is analogous to that of the consumer. He does not engineer the product, for he is no engineer. He does know what he likes, however, and on that basis purchases or refuses to purchase it.

A professional, whatever his shortcomings, must be supposed more competent than an amateur; if not, society disintegrates. One is tempted to conclude that it is for this reason that the radical student claims the "right of self-determination." Such slogans are tailor-made to rend the social fabric.

The idea of "self-determination" without qualifications has its *reductio ad absurdum*. There is no reason to deny participation in decision-making to high-school students if one grants it to college students: if qualification is eliminated as a criterion for decision-making, everyone is, by definition, qualified. Acting on this theory, 250 elementary-school children in Britain marched to the Department of Education and Science demanding "control of schools by a council of children and teachers" (London *Times*, March 3, 1969).

Reasonable people must wonder how radicals ever dug up issues which seem as ridiculous as the elimination of selective admissions, course requirements, and grades. They all follow quite logically from the thesis of absolute equality. If we were all equal, how could a university admit one person and refuse another? This would be brazen injustice. The admissions committees, moreover, would be no more qualified to make judgments about candidates for admission than those candidates themselves.

In practical terms, of course, admitting all to every university would make all universities more or less equal and would prevent any from becoming distinguished. If people who were not literate were admitted, the chances of successfully proselytizing for illiterate theories would increase, which would of course be a point for the radicals.

Certain subjects could not be taught in such a university. Literature is a discipline which, if taught on a barely literate level, is no longer literature. Calculus and physics require a certain I.Q. not attained by all. Philosophy would become a poor joke indeed if taught to people incapable of understanding abstract ideas. One wonders what, besides the social sciences would be left in such a university.

If everyone is to be admitted, course requirements must consequently be eliminated. An obvious answer! It has the additional advantage for the radical of discouraging the good student from acquiring the tools necessary for the gathering and evaluation of knowledge.

Eliminate, for example, the mathematics requirement. When the liberated student becomes a psychology major, he will read descriptions of hundreds of experiments. Most of these, in fact, are worthless: they do not establish a strong probability that the same results would not have been obtained by chance. In order to distinguish between the good and the bad experiments, he must therefore understand statistics. In order to understand statistics, he must have done a bit of math. The liberated student will thus become a psychologist incapable of distinguishing truth from error. Even with the present mathematics requirements, already considerably watered down, most new psychologists have a very hazy understanding of this very discipline—statistics—without which one accepts everything uncritically.

Eliminating the history requirement would be no wiser. Without some knowledge of what men have done and said before, one is uncritically ready to accept old ideas which have not worked. This would, of course, be perfect for radicals, who put old wine into new bottles.

The language requirement, under sharp attack by radicals at many campuses, is already so easy that students are receiving A.B.'s without being able to read a newspaper in their chosen foreign language. They are thus destined to provincialism for life. Politically, they will only see what is written in English-speaking countries and what is especially translated for them (i.e., propaganda). They will never be able to participate in foreign life or literature enough to have a real point of comparison in discussing the United States. This is another point for the radicals. When such comparisons are made, the United States comes off quite well. It is only when compared to the absolute that we look so bad.

A French-speaking person could, for example, read the *Figaro Littéraire,* in which numerous articles discussing the participation of students in decision-making have appeared recently. They are interesting in that they are not predictive but factual: student power was accepted in many French *lycées* and universities after the revolt of May, 1968. The results have been disastrous beyond imagination. The schools hardly function and little learning takes place. Instead of ending turbulence and introducing human contact, student participation in governance seems to have encouraged violence and estrangement. Such information is of obvious interest to those of us in America who are trying to assess the merits of "self-determination" for students. Its use, however, requires the knowledge of French. If one vital part of education—the language requirement—is eliminated, opposition is thereby weakened to another vital part of education: faculty rule. Eventually the rotting structure topples.

Some radicals argue that the listed requirements do correspond to worthwhile subjects (albeit somewhat "irrelevant"), but that others are just as worthwhile: sociology and food technology (their theory is that if students who are going to be in no way connected with food production nevertheless learn food technology, it will somehow save "Third-World peoples" from starvation) are named the most frequently, but the basic thesis is the absolute equality of all subjects. Radical students refuse to distinguish between disciplines giving essential tools for analysis and the gathering of knowledge and those which an *educated* person can approach alone. Philosophy is an example. If students were required to take philosophy before being allowed to take certain other subjects (e.g., psychology), they could ponder the presuppositions of these disciplines more carefully. They might never take them at all. Time would thus be saved for more significant pursuits.

The radical's desire to do away with requirements in the university is like his wish to replace the rule of law by that of his conscience. Requirements are the laws of the university. Radicals portray themselves as victims of American imperialism because their professors claim that they should learn to conjugate a few verbs. Without requirements (i.e., education) a large number of college graduates might take such rantings seriously, and we could kiss semicivilized life good-bye.

From the basic radical premise of equality, it also follows that grading should be eliminated. To be graded is to be judged by one's betters, whereas, according to this doctrine, one has no betters. In addition, the institution of grading means that certain students do better work than others. This sort of "impersonal," inhuman *"discrimination"* is under sharp attack by radicals. Indeed, certain schools (e.g., the University of California at Santa Cruz) have already eliminated grading.

The immediate result is that students are, in fact, judged (by graduate schools, employers, etc.) on the basis of letters of recommendation alone. As influence fills the vacuum created by law's exit, so personal factors replace real competence as the criterion for academic success. When a professor grades a student on a course, he averages out marks on papers and tests which he has judged on strictly professional criteria. When a letter of recommendation is to be written, many other factors come into account. The professor remembers some students better than others. Intelligent people are not always the most lovable. The result is a less just grading system. Three or four letters of recommendation are a poor substitute for thirty grades.

If the letters of recommendation were eliminated, informal phone calls would take their place, and the casual remarks of one professor would decide a student's future. In the unlikely event that radicals could end even this mode of communication, employers and graduate schools would institute their own testing. If, through some oppressive technique, radicals eliminated even this, employers and graduate schools would select candidates on the basis of chance alone: the quality of every undertaking in America would of course plummet. Is this not the radical goal?

Anyone who has his doubts should consider another radical

demand: the sharp reduction and eventual elimination of work
in the university. Doing away with grading would remove the
prime incentive to work. Very few people would work as hard
for the love of knowledge as for grades. Grades are the pay
system in the university. Eliminate pay and you have eliminated hard work. One need look no further than the kolkhozes
and factories of the Soviet Union to realize that incentives are
indispensable.

In most universities today a student may take one course a
semester on a Pass-Fail basis. This means that one grade will
not appear on his transcript. If he receives a C or better, he is
given a Pass. In some universities a grade of D is sufficient.
In effect one course is eliminated as a candidate for serious
work. For radicals, this is only the beginning. They are pushing
for the next step: instead of receiving a grade of Pass or Fail,
they want to receive a Pass if they have a C, but to have *no
record made at all* if they fail! They also wish to be allowed to
take an unlimited number of courses on a Pass-No Record basis.
This would mean that the student could do practically no work,
for half the time none is necessary to obtain a C, not to mention
a D. To obtain credit for five courses, for example, he could
enroll in ten, do nothing except take the final exam, and come
up with five Passes.

Pressure has also been successfully applied by radicals to reduce the total number of courses required. The usual technique
is to insist that the number of credits awarded for each course
be increased. If, for example, twelve units of credit are required each semester and an average course gives three, the
student must take four courses (3 x 4 equals 12). If the unit
credit for each course is raised to four, however, only three
courses need be taken. This has already been done on many
campuses in the United States. Three courses, one on a Pass-
Fail basis, one perhaps in Tutoring in the Community, and
one in sociology (623 studies proving that Southerners dislike Negroes) can fulfill the student's obligations to the world
of science and letters. Is it really any wonder that so much noise
is heard on our campuses?

Among the other targets of student radicals are ROTC and
government research grants made to university professors.
Underpinning radical stands on these matters is the supposition
that the university is so biased in favor of the American system ("imperialism, racism, capitalism") that it cannot give an
impartial education. This supposition is itself an issue dear
to radicals. They demand that all bias be removed, as it is in-
compatible with "real" education. This issue could never be
resolved so as to satisfy radicals. Regardless what concessions
they won through agitation, there would always be something
American about American universities. If the no-bias rule were
to be followed to its surreal conclusion, American food could
not be served in university cafeterias: profits from its sale serve
to perpetuate the system and suppress "Third-World peoples"
all over the globe. American buildings could not be used, for
builders make profits, workers make wages, and they all pay
taxes into the nefarious system. American professors could not
be hired, for they are products of our society and co-operate with
it. No professors could be paid unless they promised to break
the law and withhold their taxes. Even if such things could
be done, the no-bias principle would nevertheless be violated:
education would be severely slanted against the "system."

Once it is admitted that all partiality should be removed, there
can be no peace. Academic freedom itself can be seen as
partiality. As the American "system" is essentially free, to allow
freedom in the universities is to apply American bias. Eliminate
academic freedom, however, and you have, by definition, an
official slant towards one type of slavery or another. The bias towards freedom is consequently the least amount of bias possible
in an educational system.

Where bias towards the system really counts and can, in
fact, corrupt education is in the classroom. It is here that nobody
of good faith could say that there is pro-American slant. It is
academic freedom, that "bourgeois lie," that permits professors
to denounce what they dislike in America every day. Many of
those who publicly express their desire to tear down the university and American society, such people as Lichtman and Marcuse, are in the university. Some of the Regents of the University
of California, it is true, wanted to fire Marcuse, just as he wishes

to get rid of his enemies. It is our "biased" system which prevented his departure, as it has since prevented that of his disciple Angela Davis.

We have seen that the American professor is more alienated from the system than almost anyone else in America. Students almost always move left in the university, which is, according to radicals, the right direction. The only causes radicals have for complaint are that professors usually stop short of fanaticism and that moderate views are not outlawed.

The university is completely unbiased—except in that it is for freedom—on the essential matters: each professor is allowed to say exactly what he wishes in class and to choose his own research. Professors also play the predominant role in determining university policies on requirements, credits, and courses. In addition, American universities make every effort to allow their students to gain further perspective by a year of schooling abroad. The larger "American system" provides the money for such ventures.

The radical's call for an end to bias is therefore ridiculous. Moreover, it contradicts another tenet of his creed. He believes that bias cannot be removed until society is completely transformed (e.g., Mark Rudd, *New York Times,* August 4, 1968). He is therefore demanding what he recognizes as impossible. When he denounces ROTC or links between government and the university, he is in contradiction with his idea of changing society first. He is consistent, however, with his real goal of destroying the system by destroying the university.

ROTC is the radical's best case on its merits. Its basic purpose is military rather than academic. ROTC in the university can, of course, be defended on the ground that the university has a special interest in the preservation of freedom. It is obvious that without an American military apparatus, we professors would be obliged, like our Czechoslovakian colleagues, to teach official propaganda. It can also be said in defense of ROTC that the information on waging war obtained by taking it need not be used to defend the United States. Exit from this country is free, and nobody can stop enemies of America from using their military knowledge against it. It must also be mentioned that very few colleges require students to take ROTC. The radical attitude is, however, that no one should be *allowed* to take it, just as nobody should be allowed to express reactionary, racist, or militant views. Although against course requirements, radicals wish to introduce a negative requirement against courses distasteful to them. Freedom is not for the pigs.

Academic credit for certain parts of the ROTC program, such as drill, is of course indefensible. But no more so than that awarded for tutoring in the community, sports, giving information on the telephone, and the myriad other "subjects" which are not being attacked by radicals. If all subjects are equal (the argument used against requirements), so is ROTC. If grades, selective admissions, and requirements should be eliminated, there are no academic standards. From this it can be deduced that the academic argument is for professorial consumption alone. It is the line of reasoning which professors find the most respectable and the best excuse for giving in to radicals.

ROTC programs are now doomed in the best American universities. It remains to be seen whether their demise will usher in a period of idyllic peace on the campuses. What is certain is that the number of liberally educated, civilian-oriented American military officers will be lower in the future. This will not, as radicals believe, prevent America from waging war. It will remove from positions of responsibility in the armed forces those most likely to speak out against the idea that might makes right—i.e., against unfair treatment of the private, the torturing of prisoners of war, and contempt for civil authority.

Co-operation between government and the university is an issue on which radicals seem particularly illogical. They are in favor of the nationalization, i.e., government ownership, of everything. Therefore, the closer government gets to the university, the happier they should be. Instead, they take the ultraconservative view that there should be no links of any kind between government and the university.

There is nothing, in any case, reprehensible about the present system. A professor wishes to do research on a given subject. He applies for funds from all available sources, among which are governmental agencies. If his research coincides with the national interest, he will receive federal aid. Government represents the people and the people obviously have the right to decide how they want to spend their money. The professor's duty is to do his work as best he can with the funds he has. The government never forces a person to do research on any subject: it is powerless to do so. The radical thesis that the government, because it holds the purse strings, dictates what shall be studied and what shall not be studied, is absolutely false. Because it is only one source of financial support among many (and because federal monies are disbursed through several channels), very few research projects proposed by people whom their peers respect are rejected for want of funds. If one looks into the projects of radical professors, I am sure one will find that they too have received the necessary financial assistance for their work. Marcuse's *One-Dimensional Man,* a poorly reasoned critique of free enterprise, was partially financed by the Rockefeller Foundation!

One of the most absurd aspects of the radicals' insistence on the elimination of bias in education is that it contradicts their most important demand: that the university seek good, help exploited people, and oppose imperialism, racism and capitalism. On the one hand radicals are saying that the university should be absolutely neutral and on the other that it should be deliberately biased—in favor, of course, of their theories.

A recent article by Sidney Hook discusses in detail the radical idea of a political university, interested, not in truth, but in good.[1] It quotes Richard Lichtman as saying that "a free and human community of scholars can only flourish when the multitudinous communities of the exploited, the wretched, and the brutalized peoples of the earth have broken the bonds of their subservience and established themselves as men of full stature" (p. 466). Until such time, the university should, according to Lichtman, be devoted to political action rather than disinterested scholarship. Academic freedom is a "platitude" to be disposed of. "Until men of knowledge act to change

[1] Hook, Sidney, "The Barbarism of Virtue." *Publications of the Modern Language Association of America,* March, 1969.

the world, they cannot claim the unrestrained right to understand it" (p. 472). In order to see whether this radical proposition is valid, let us apply it to itself. Lichtman means either than none of us has acted "to change the world" or that some of us have. If, as is probably the case, he means that none of us has, it follows that none of us can claim the right to understand it. Lichtman supposedly understands what he is saying; otherwise, how can he claim that it is true? Yet, according to his own proposition, he has no right to do so. He is therefore obliged to use his machinery of repression against himself.

Perhaps, however, he means that some people have, in fact, acted to change the world, and that they are the ones who have the right to understand it. Who are they? We can all claim that we are acting to change the world. How do we distinguish between the legitimate and the illegitimate claims? Whatever method we use, in trying to find out who is entitled to *understand*, i.e., to seek the truth, we are seeking the *truth* of the matter—a false answer to the question would, of course, be useless. But how can we seek the truth of any matter before we know if we are entitled to do so? How dare we attempt to understand who is allowed to understand? Lichtman's proposition interpreted the first way is contradictory. Interpreted the second way, it is inapplicable. Both ways it is nonsense.

Carl Schorske, another radical professor, puts the same sort of restriction on the search for truth, but employs a different New Left sophism: "Has the right to pursue the truth wherever it leads a more absolute justification than the right to pursue free enterprise wherever it leads?" (quoted by Hook, p. 470). This is very confused thinking indeed. The poor fellow mixes up free thought and free enterprise because the first word of each is "free"! He concludes that they are therefore the same sort of thing. Sidney Hook, who is a patient man, discusses the assertion at length before refuting it through an analysis of its consequences. One could furthermore ask Schorske if he is speaking truth or falsehood. If falsehood, he is wasting our time. If truth, he is unjustified in speaking, since, he contends, the pursuit of truth is no more justifiable than that of commerce. It goes without saying that he does not think free enterprise justifiable at all.

Indeed, the issue is absurd, for how can one *know* what is

good without some criterion for knowledge? When one says that
morality is a better goal than truth, is it true? If the statement is not proven on the basis of truth, how can one accept
it? The acceptance of truth as the ultimate arbiter is the *sine
qua non* of any discussion on any matter. Deciding what is good
is the concern of ethics, which depends on metaphysics, which
in turn depends on epistemology. All are branches of philosophy,
which is the systematic search for . . . truth. All propositions
(statements) contain the implicit assertion, "This is true."
Without this assertion, what would the proposition be, but so
much slop? One cannot even say, "This is slop," without implying that it is *true* that it is slop.

A university is an institution for the discovery and dissemina-
tion of truth. If interested, as an institution, in anything else,
it is no longer a university, for the other goals, whatever they
may be, will eventually clash with truth. There is no point in discussing this last assertion further as Hook's excellent article is
devoted to demonstrating it.

It is the idea of the political university, seeking good, which
has been used to bolster Black Studies programs. The university
must correct the inequities of society by admitting blacks who
are not qualified. It is a question of reparations. First, America
owes reparations to blacks for the years of racism. This principle
itself has its dangers. What group cannot claim it has been discriminated against? American Italians, Germans, Irishmen, Jews,
Indians, Chinese and Japanese all could legitimately militate for
their share of reparations. Many Anglo-Saxon Protestants claim
that at present it is they who are being discriminated against.
If, through a perverted devotion to absolute justice, they are all
to be indemnified, chaos will surely reign. Will the majority of
Americans vote to make reparations—in either money or preferential treatment—to any of these groups? I doubt it. Democracy will therefore have to disappear in the interest of Justice.

To whom will the reparations be made? Those who suffered
discrimination are, for the most part, either old or dead. Does
one inherit the right to reparations? Are members of groups
once discriminated against to be collectively innocent as "soci-

ety" is collectively guilty? Radicals apparently think so.

If these reparations were made, those making them would become the new victims of injustice. The white student deserving admission to a university who is turned down in favor of a less qualified black has been done an injustice. His sons forever more, according to the reparation principle, could claim reparations. There is a pertinent old saw to the effect that two wrongs do not make a right.

Another claim made for preferential admissions is that, because blacks have been segregated from white society, they have had inferior training. Their scholastic record is therefore no indication of their native ability. The answer is of course that junior colleges and special programs to prepare blacks for college are necessary.

What is surprising is to find that the radicals have foisted on the blacks an "answer" to this problem which is a continuation and an exacerbation of it. The basic presupposition, that blacks have suffered from segregation, implies that the very worst thing they could do would be to militate for segregated Black Studies programs. Rather than catching up, blacks would fall further behind—according to the radicals' presuppositions.

It must be remembered that one article of the radical's credo is the absurd assumption that America is the most racist country in the world. His solution to the problem is to segregate blacks from whites once they arrive in college. Now if I shared the radicals' conspiratorial theory of history, would I not say—with a great deal of verisimilitude—that we have here a cynical plot to divide Americans in order to conquer them? As long as blacks are in Black Studies programs they will be badly educated (according to the radicals' presupposition). Reason will therefore not reign in the black community; blacks will not rise in society. Integration and the accompanying equal-status contact which mitigates prejudices will be halted. Blacks will remain discontented and will become more and more the tools of SDS and like radical groups.

Some radicals probably do think of themselves as clever exploiters of Negroes. Most, however, are not conspiring. They are simply victims of sloppy thinking who sincerely believe they are helping blacks. They refuse to see that there can never be a community of interest between a group trying to get a piece of the action and another trying to break up the game.

Black Studies are not to be condemned. They are, in fact, part of American Studies. Area studies, including African, already exist in many universities. The radical genius has shown itself, not in asking for Black Studies courses, but in convincing many black students that Black Studies Centers should be entirely separate from the rest of the university. All students and teachers would be black. They would have segregated living quarters. And, since the radicals have added their idea of student dominance to the plans for black colleges, the students would hire and fire their professors and thus be the ultimate authorities on all matters.

In addition to being illegal, this is a perfect recipe for racial hatred and an apartheid unlike any seen in the northern states of America since the nineteenth century. For how could people who had spent four segregated years "learning" from teachers of their own choosing fit into white society? There is nothing more conducive to hatred and suspicion among races than proximity without contact. Blacks would come from college ready to kill whites. White racists would be only too eager to retaliate. The minority of radicals lucid enough to know this think perhaps that they would then unfurl their banners and "liberate" America.

A radical issue which has gained popularity with many non-radicals is relevance. The cry for relevance is used to defend Black Studies. The culture taught in the university is white. Blacks are black. Therefore all studies in the university are irrelevant to blacks! This delirious syllogism is based on the confusion between two uses of the word "culture." Traditionally, "culture" means the highest achievements in the arts, sciences, letters, and thought. An allied meaning of the term is the knowledge held by an individual of these great achievements. A person who has knowledge of the arts and sciences is cultured. "American culture" would simply mean the superior works produced by Americans. "White culture" would be the superior works of whites. Since we are all human, however, it really does not matter to us *who* produced the work. What counts is the work itself. Whatever its origin, if it is a masterpiece, it comes to belong to *world culture*. What students in universities are taught is world culture, neither black nor white. To say otherwise is to affirm that Arab discoveries in mathematics are irrelevant to American math, that "Jewish physics" is irrelevant to science in the *Vaterland*, or that "Bach was just a honkey pig."

The other meaning of "culture," which radicals fail to distinguish from the traditional one, is sociological. The sum total of ways of living built up by a group of people is a "culture." The study of groups has itself become an academic discipline. It is not to be implied, however, that the study of "culture" (i.e., groups) has made all other studies (culture) obsolete. If one is going to study groups, there is no reason why black Americans should not be studied. Indeed they already have been. To imply, however, that all other studies but the study of one's own group are irrelevant, is absurd. The radical argument that by learning world culture blacks are giving up black "culture" (i.e., the ways of living of blacks) is for the same reason absurd. A member of a black "culture" (group) who becomes educated is now a cultured member of that group. To say that to be cultured is no longer to be black is to affirm that the nature of blackness is to be uncultured. In short, it is virulent racism.

The radicals who cry out that American education is irrelevant are again contradicting themselves. Do they not also state that the educational system is designed to perpetuate the evil capitalistic system? If that is so, it is obviously not irrelevant.

"Irrelevant to what?" is the question one would like to ask them. If they mean to their immediate interests—food, shelter, and sex—they are asking for a trade-school approach. Education is, after all, teaching people things which are not so obviously related to their personal lives that they would see the link by themselves.

Truth is the goal of the university. Reasoned debate in the university concerns truth, good, and beauty. Are these irrelevant? If our student is extravagant enough to say "yes," he must mean that it is *true* that truth is irrelevant. If he is right, he is irrelevant.

What radicals may well really mean (one can never be sure) is that education is irrelevant to revolution. Therefore we should have a revolution to get rid of the irrelevance. The argument is a perfect circle. The goal of revolution justifies the complaints about irrelevance and the irrelevance justifies the revolution.

Rationalists are dangerous men from the radical point of view. They follow their reasoning wherever it leads, even if what Lichtman calls "the party of humanity" is hurt. "Relevance" is, at its most pernicious, the code word warning against such objectivity. Its function is to remind people that they must ask themselves whether a statement will help the radical cause before making it. If not, it is "irrelevant," regardless how true.

Often the complaints about irrelevance seem to be simply a pretentious way of expressing one's boredom. If we are to dignify our distastes by calling the people and the topics that do not interest us "irrelevant," I may as well call politics irrelevant. In my opinion, the real problems of man—salvation, death, the right path in life—are not susceptible to political solutions. Therefore politics is irrelevant. In like manner, someone else could say that the concept of relevance itself is irrelevant.

For the radical there is an emotional link between the issue of relevance and that of depersonalization. Perhaps it is because in both cases he seeks the bread of emotional experience whereas teachers give him the stone that is reason. Reason is itself impersonal in that it cannot be twisted to conform to one's desires. That is why people often show a marked preference for illogical thinking: it makes answers come out right for the emotions.

When asked to explain how the university could become relevant, students often suggest that all subjects should cohere—i.e., that professors should give them a total explanation of the world. Cries against depersonalization imply that this coherent picture should change one's life and make it beautiful. This is howling for the moon, an innocent if unprofitable activity. To assert that it is the fault of the American system when the moon is not obtained, however, is either foolish or wicked.

Knowledge is divided into subjects difficult to relate to each other, not because the capitalists wish to mock idealistic American youth, but because each discipline has its own logic. Knowledge is fragmented at present because it is limited. We would all like to find a meaningful synthesis of everything that is known. Indeed, this is the goal of metaphysics.

To blame capitalism for the fact that no answer which can stand the test of reason has been found is like blaming it for death. To accept, like the radicals, a false synthesis which reduces everything to political terms is to preclude the finding of that very synthesis which radicals desire. For once you convince yourself that you have the solution, you need look no further. Consequently, the answer to depersonalization in life and in the university will not be found by irrational sloganeering, by radical "demands" and "confrontations" which divide humanity into "pigs" and the "people," or by the refusal to deal with any issue on less than a "groupuscule" level, but, if at all, by serious reflection.

All of the issues discussed here unite the same students. Whether it be Viet Nam, language requirements, or ROTC, it is the same core group which opposes what is being done by the university. Is it possible for the same people to have independently arrived at the same absurd conclusions on all these issues? It is in any case most improbable. It would not be completely unjustified to conclude that there is, as I have implied throughout this discussion, a certain regrettable cynicism on the part of radicals toward these very issues which they themselves have brought forward. One has the impression that many of the issues are pretexts for violence rather than causes of it.

3

FALSE SOLUTIONS

It is beyond the scope of this work to explain in detail why supposedly qualified people have proposed obviously false solutions to the problem of campus violence. The causes mentioned in the first chapter are applicable to the professor and administrator (usually a former professor). For both the politician and the professor the cult of change is an additional factor. The desirability of change is one radical thesis which is as traditionally American as apple pie. Whatever is, is already old-fashioned.

If there is violence on our campuses, the obvious American answer would therefore be to change something. What can be changed in a university? Certain subjects (e.g., literature and philosophy) do not change in nature. The methods of studying them cannot be radically improved: to learn philosophy, the student reads and thinks. If this were changed, he would no longer be learning philosophy. Other subjects—the sciences and all applied skills—change rapidly. In the teaching of these the university has changed, and is constantly changing its methods. Do we not have the new math, new physics, and case-book law? A third type of discipline does not change much in content but can be taught more effectively with newer methods. Languages, for example, are reasonably stable whereas methods of teaching them are subject to change. These methods, in fact, do change. Do we not have the audio-lingual method and an ever growing literature on language instruction? It would seem, then, that the university has not committed the grievous sin of dissent from the Cult of Change. Wherever appropriate, innovation has been eagerly accepted. The only fundamental change possible in this area would therefore be to stop changing. Since no one wishes to do this, another area for change must be found.

Improvements can of course always be made in buildings and classrooms. In Europe, complaints about inadequate facilities are often made by student radicals to gain the sympathy of moderates. They have a legitimate issue. Such is obviously not the case in the United States, where facilities are not only adequate but frequently sumptuous.

Would it be possible to change the number of students admitted to our universities? In Europe, radicals demand the democratization of their universities, which have traditionally admitted less than 10 per cent of college-age youth. Those admitted are overwhelmingly from the wealthiest families. There is therefore some merit (although less than five years ago) to the accusation that the university is of and for the privileged. Transported to America, where over 50 per cent of high-school graduates attend a university, the accusation becomes absurd. The only academically feasible change possible here would be a reduction in the number of students, and this would please few people.

Could professors be made to "relate" better to their students? In Europe, radicals bitterly denounced the "magistral course" in which, they claimed, there was virtually no contact between professor and student. Even in France and in Germany, this was an exaggeration. In the United States, where professors go to great lengths to be good guys whose doors and ears are always open, the criticism is ridiculous.

Changes in the basic American institutions which the radicals abhor—free speech, checks and balances in government, free elections, and private property—have no relation to the university and can only be made (legally) by elected public officials. It would seem, from the amount of support the Peace and Freedom Party received during the 1968 elections, that eliminating violence in the university by legally altering the structure of society is not practicable.

What must therefore be changed, if change one must, are the university's work load, grading system, governance, admissions policy, etc.—the very matters on which radicals have a blueprint for change.

Can changes in the very areas which interest radicals be made exactly contrary to radical demands? This would be provocation. If, on the other hand, modifications were made which brought the university closer to the radical dream, would this not show a healthy confidence in youth which would end violence? Radicals would realize that the United States is not so horrible after all and we should all live happily—and peacefully—ever after.

This is the first and foremost of the false solutions to violence: granting concessions to radicals. This sort of "reform" has been suggested by innumerable politicians, journalists, professors and administrators of all political persuasions. Senator Abraham Ribicoff, a liberal Democrat, has offered the following solutions to student violence: "a real working student council" (i.e., partial self-determination for students), government efforts to "get to work on many of the social reforms advocated by college youth" (an end to free speech, the political university, and non-selective admissions?), and the realization by society that "youthful dissatisfaction is not destructive but a determination to make sure the world's richest nation provides for its poor as well as its rich, its black as well as white" (by supporting segregated Black Studies programs?). These words appeared in a UPI dispatch of June 9, 1969. Governor Ronald Reagan, a conservative Republican, has stated that "the students' legitimate grievances must be understood and solutions must be forthcoming." It is clearly implied here, as it is not by some liberals, that not all student grievances are legitimate. But it is also clear that to Reagan many are. Although there are, in fact, a few legitimate student grievances (e.g., they are being deprived of their education by radical agitation), they are not those of the radicals. Hubert Humphrey has summed up the theory of reform in the most general and innocent-sounding way: "It is critically important that students support reform—non-violent reform." The President's panel on violence has declared that the United States must "carry through a firm commitment to massive and widespread reform." For all of them, the answer to violence is reform.

This solution is based on two unfortunate confusions. First, the people quoted fail to distinguish between a university and the government of the United States. It is by analogy with third parties that their urgings to reform are made. They see the students as a third party which will disappear in the traditional American way when its platform is adopted by the major parties. The second confusion takes place inside the first. Even if American government and the university were comparable, the analogy would be misleading. The third party platforms adopted by the major parties were popular, whereas radical programs for the university are as unpopular as their programs for society as a whole. This is not surprising, for it is the radical dogma as it pertains to issues outside the university that determines radical demands on academic matters.

The advocates of reform are not, however, confused on this point alone. It must be supposed that they either think they should make concessions to the radicals even though they are wrong, or that they agree to some extent with radical stands on the issues. Both possibilities are a bit frightening. In the first case, we have appeasement, a bid for peace at any price— even the destruction of the university. In the second, we can only assume that many leaders think no more clearly than the radicals themselves.

For example, Kingman Brewster Jr., president of Yale University, goes along with the radical idea that we should expect absolute perfection of the United States. He also agrees with its corollary: if we do not have perfection, violence is, if not justified, at least excusable. For him reform on a national scale is needed to bring peace to the university: "campus violence will grow worse unless an intense effort is made to end the war in Vietnam, remove the inequities in the draft, solve the problems of the cities and improve race relations." (*Time*, May 16, 1969). In short, the answer to violence is to be found in perfection: when the United States becomes a province of Paradise, radicals will be content and agitate no more. Until such time, anything goes. Whether the president of Yale is attempting to appease radicals or sincerely sympathizes with their goals and methods, the effect is the same. The blame for violence is shifted from those committing it to Society.

Reformist sentiments such as these have already brought about many changes on campus. It is for this reason that we can see whether concessions on such issues as the elimination of grading, work, course requirements, selective admissions, and faculty rule, whatever their intrinsic merits, do bring peace to the university. Radical demands have already been partially satisfied on the following issues: the work load (reduced), grading (Pass-Fail courses in many schools, complete elimination of grading in a few), admissions (standards have been lowered for blacks), requirements (reduced), ROTC (on its last legs), Black Studies (being instituted everywhere, but rarely segregated), and student power (advisory role almost everywhere, minority voting power in many colleges, majority voting power at Goddard College). The university has grown more violent while these concessions were being made. The reasons are obvious. First, the changes prove to radicals that violence pays. Second, radical students have not yet attained all their objectives. As soon as one step is made, there is the next. The ultimate step, the only one which will satisfy radicals, is the step to absolute power. The rioting at Harvard in the spring of 1969 is a case in point. Radicals made several demands, including the selection of the head of the new Afro-American department by black students (i.e., self-determination) and the construction of housing units for low and moderate-income families (i.e., the political university). Harvard capitulated to these and all other demands made. It thereby gravely compromised its academic standards. Nevertheless, the result has not been peace and goodwill. At the beginning of the next (fall) semester, radicals "demanded" that the Center for International Affairs be shut down and announced their intention to invade it.

The demand for Black Studies caused so much violence that programs have sprung up all over. Have black radicals become less violent? Incidents at Cornell, Brandeis, Swarthmore, and dozens of other schools say no. Norman Sklarewitz interviewed many of the students and faculty members participating in the fledgling Black Studies program at Stanford (*Wall Street Journal*, June 11, 1969). The Negro head of the program, James L. Gibbs Jr., stated that Stanford's blacks were "action-orientated." Volunteer students conduct extracurricular sessions which, according to him, damage the opportunity for thoughtful dialogue between students and instructor. He feels that students finish the course with the same misconceptions they had before taking it. Protest actions have not diminished since the program's inception, and more than ten major new demands have been made at Stanford.

What these two examples prove is that radicals can fabricate new issues and new demands faster than universities can capitulate. To think otherwise is to accept, in the face of evidence to the contrary, two radical suppositions: (1) that man is very good, and (2) that the radical is angelic. If radicals were the idealistic, fair-minded youths they and many others say they are, concessions might work. They would regard them as a sign of goodwill and abandon violence. The same is true in international affairs. If men were good, we could unilaterally disarm, and our Chinese and Russian brothers would hasten to do the same.

As the radicals believe, or say that they believe, in such things, one is not surprised to see that they usually imply that if their "just demands" were met, violence would end. They are not, of course, in favor of unilateral disarmament for themselves. They would first have to get what they wanted. Then they would smoke the pipe of peace. Even if they were sincere in saying this, however, the bad solutions they offer to cure the ills of America would produce further violence. Each solution would breed new, and much greater problems—whence new demands, new violence, and new solutions ad infinitum. One former leader of the Free Speech Movement at Berkeley inadvertently let the cat out of the bag in an interview with Thomas B. Carter (*Wall Street Journal*, June 4, 1969): "They [the people in power] haven't figured out what's wrong yet. They're asking, 'What can we give these kids to keep them quiet?' I'll tell you what. A new society, that's what. You can't contain this by buying it off with a few Black Studies programs." Indeed! After reading this confession, it becomes clear that concessions are not the solution but a large part of the problem.

One of the greatest encouragements to radicals is that they seem to be admired by representatives of the very institutions they wish to destroy: politicians, teachers, and administrators. Calling radicals idealists may seem to be conciliatory wisdom, but it is a cause of further violence. Even psychologists know that people, especially the irrational and unintelligent, tend to do what brings approval.

When changes are made in response to violence, and always in the direction demanded by those committing it, radicals conclude that society not only agrees with them on the issues but condones violence for a good cause. As this is tantamount to granting permission to be radical, it adds new converts to radicalism. Concessions, consequently, set up the university for the next outbreak of violence. Let us say that a given university has had confrontations over the issue of Black Studies and that the administration building has been stormed. The police are not called and a program is promptly set up which satisfies about half the demands made. A month later, a military recruiter comes to the campus. Radicals claim that he should not be allowed free speech because "the military deprives people of life and free speech," or something to that effect. They smash up the student placement office (this happened at Columbia) and threaten further violence. Can the university call the police to protect lives and property? How can it justify doing so now if it did not do so the last time? The situation is the same: violation of the law. If the university does not cave in to more demands, it is now obliged to use greater force to restore order than would have been necessary before. More people have espoused violence in the last month because of its success. Nobody expects the police to be called. If the university does so, it is now the oppressor, for it is acting inconsistently. It has already been established by precedent that violence is tolerated. The university, in calling the police, is breaking its word. Even non-radical students are indignant. In a sense they are right: institutions devoted to reason should not act illogically.

The university is obliged at this point either to submit to a reign of terror or to "repress" a large and self-righteous crowd. The more the university concedes, the bloodier will be the final act, which will be played out when even administrators and professors realize they can yield no more.

To adopt radical ideas would thus be foolhardy, not only be-

cause they are wrong, but because new "ideas" and new violence would be the result. Concessions are not only a false solution to violence but a cause of fresh violence.

The other false solution is voiced by very few people of influence. It is the "repression" which, according to radicals, already exists. True repression would consist in the university's
depriving students of their legal rights. If student newspapers
and radio stations were rigorously censored as to political content, this would be repression. If growing beards and spout-
ing nonsense on college quads were forbidden, this would be
repression. If *legal* dissent were outlawed, this would be repression. If a political test for professors were introduced, this
would be repression.

The few in favor of such measures argue that students are
not in universities to agitate but to learn. Learning, however,
presupposes the free exchange of opinions. Obviously, the institution of free speech cannot be protected by depriving others
of it; if it is not for all, it is, by definition, not free speech.

The idea of a political test for professors is defended by some
on the grounds that there already is *de facto* political discrimination in favor of ultra-liberals on campus. Such a test would
therefore not, they reason, be like that of the radical Lichtman,
which would eliminate *all* those who disagree with him. It
would restore political balance to the faculty and would thus
be favorable to free speech rather than harmful to it.

Although it is true that there is some pro-liberal discrimination
in faculties, this remedy is worse than the disease. It is a bit
like the radical idea of a quota system by which blacks would
have the same percentage of positions in the university as there
are blacks in the population. One wonders whether a staff
made up of 50 per cent Democrats and 50 per cent Republicans
(or whatever figures the latest election showed) would be as
good as one picked freely, and what the liberals deprived of
positions they deserved would say. Reagan and the radicals are
both thinking in terms of a dubious justice to one type of group
(conservatives, blacks) at the expense of justice, not only to
other groups (the general public, students), but to *individuals*

(liberals or white students qualified but refused because of a quota system).

A certain amount of discrimination against conservatives must be accepted as inevitable in the university. To discriminate is unfortunately a part of human nature. To ask for perfection would be to repeat the radical assertion that only perfection is acceptable. More important, neither government nor the university can sponsor discrimination: an official quota system designed to correct the wrongs of an unofficial one merely worsens a bad situation. The criterion of merit is completely lost in the shuffle.

There is no empirical proof, of course, that repression could not quell radical violence. Unlike concessions to radicals, it has not been tried on American campuses. It has, however, been used in other situations over the last three thousand years—with violent results. Indeed, it is a basic American principle that repression is the one and only justification for violence.

Yielding to absurd demands and depriving radicals of their rights are thus equally unfair and unwise. Neither is a solution to violence. Both are more likely to cause it.

4

TRUE SOLUTIONS

The first obvious solution to violence is to withdraw the tacit permission for it. Americans have traditionally condemned violence as indefensible in a democracy. As long as people have their rights, it is always illegitimate. These rights are minutely defined in law. In order that others may not interfere with them, other laws have been passed forbidding certain acts—assault and battery, arson, etc. Now, however, people in important positions refer to this second type of law as "negative." James E. Allen, U. S. Commissioner of Education, has said that problems in education cannot be solved "by passing punitive or negative legislation" (UPI, May 19, 1969). He was referring to bills forbidding such acts as forcibly preventing a professor from teaching his class.

If the laws are "negative," does this not imply that the acts they prevent are positive, or at least permissible? Laws against violence are negative. Violence may consequently be committed.

With just a bit sloppier thinking, a "right" to violence can be claimed. A law student at the University of California at Davis develops the theme with touching naïveté in the local newspaper. Students, he opines, were wholly unable to influence those factors which determined their education." This was wrong! "Finally the students' request for the right to participate in the development of curricula; to participate in the selection of research programs; to participate in the selection of community service projects; to participate in the determination of course content, in the selection of faculty and administrators—turned to demands. Students desire and are demanding a meaningful voice in the legitimate affairs of the school. When student demands, like their requests, were rejected—they staged sit-ins, teach-ins and other forms of civil disobedience" (*Davis*

76

Enterprise, June 2, 1969). By these "other forms of civil disobedience" he means, of course, violence. That is about all that is left. His reasoning is easy enough to decompose: student self-determination is right. Peaceful means were tried, but they did not work. Therefore violence was justified, for—this is the premise—the end justifies the means. He concludes that the solution to violence is for the professors to give equal power to students!

It is not only radical students who feel that violence is not absolutely wrong if committed for a just cause. A relativistic generation hesitates to condemn anything absolutely. The principal argument used in favor of violence is that it hastens change. Much is said about the slowness of legal change. In fact, the number of changes brought about by law in the last twenty years is incredible. In 1950, "separate but equal" was the civil rights law of the land. The guarantees of the Bill of Rights applied only to the federal government's relation to individuals. Some states had no Bill of Rights in their constitutions and could consequently flout the individual's basic rights. The accused could often be interrogated without a lawyer. Confessions extracted by mental—and sometimes even physical— pressure were not uncommon. The death penalty was applied, not only for murder, but for rape.

All of these shortcomings have been corrected without student violence. Negro violence came well after the major civil rights laws and was therefore not necessary to attain them.

The accusation of legal slowness is therefore false. Even if it were true, however, it would not prove that violence is permissible. It would indicate rather that the people of America are in favor of slow change. To say that they must be forced to change quickly to do "right" is to claim infallibility for oneself and deny the principles of democratic government.

"Violence" has as its general meaning "swift and intense force." As applied to the acts of human beings it is "rough or *injurious* physical force, action, or treatment." In a political situation it is "an *unjust* or *unwarranted* exertion of force or power, as against *rights, laws,* etc." (*The Random House Dictionary of the English Language.* Italics are mine.) In a democracy, violence is used only by a minority incapable of convincing others by argument (if it could persuade, it would gain its objectives by the vote) and fanatically convinced of its infallibility. As it relates to issues in the university, violence is rejection of faculty rule, and thus of education. As it pertains to general politics, violence is rejection of majority rule and thus of democracy.

This commonplace plainly wants repeating, for SDS states that it is a champion of "participatory democracy." One would think that this means that SDS is for the vote if one did not know how it defines "people." Democracy is rule by the people and the "people," we have seen, are those who agree with SDS (the others are "pigs"). Therefore to have "democracy" it is necessary to have "participation," which means, of course, to have violence.

It would be useful to distinguish sharply between the legal and the illegal use of force. The former is implied by laws granting rights and forbidding specific acts interfering with them. If laws were not *enforced*, they would be meaningless. Man would have no more rights, for there would be no way of preventing others from taking them away. The illegal use of force on the other hand, merits the term "violence" by definition.

Sentiment against violence is still very strong in the United States. Only the most rabid groups (SDS, Black Panthers, etc.) support it wholeheartedly. Even the law student whose attempt to establish a right to violence was quoted felt constrained to use the euphemism "other forms of civil disobedience." Radicals who retain some well-hidden doubts about the "Movement" usually combine a cursory parroting of the credo (violence to destroy a society as horrible as ours is permissible) with an attempt to attach the "violent" label to the victims of violence.

This can easily be done to people who never analyze. Kenneth Rexroth, for example, solemnly tells radicals that "the initiation of violence does not come from your side. Don't let the demagogues tell you that you are on the offensive. You are not. Blacks—students—all along the line have been attacked, not the other way around" (*El Gaucho*, May 28, 1969). He concludes by stating that society is getting ready to put all protestors into concentration camps! This is an exhortation to new self-righteousness, condemnation of society and violence: why restrain oneself against Gross Nasty Pig, who locks people up?

It should be noticed that nowhere in his remarks does Rexroth attempt to prove what he says. He contents himself with guru-like affirmation. John Kenneth Galbraith is equally authoritarian when stating (in a commencement address) that recent violence at Harvard "was commanded not by those who were guilty [of taking over buildings], but by those who spoke most unctuously against it. It was they and not the students who induced the action that cracked the heads." In short, violence is caused by those who speak against it (especially with unction), not by those who perpetrate it. Galbraith has simply changed the word's definition. For him, if it is illegal, it is not violence. The legal use of persuasion, however, is violence and is therefore bad. Dictionaries, of course, tend to see things the other way around: the warranted use, not only of persuasion, but of force is not violence; it is only force "against rights, laws, etc." which merits that term. By changing the definition, radicals hope to put the onus attached to the word "violence" on those who attempt to stop violence. It is "only" a question of language, but very important. All of the disapproval the word evokes is now attached to those who are not, by normal definition, violent. The true offenders are let off the hook and encouraged to commit further violence. Definitions are, of course, free. If one wishes to define "violence" in a political situation as *any* use of force, legitimate or not, one has the right to do so. In this case, the onus attached to the illegitimate use of force should not be associated with the word "violence." An honest writer would point out that the horror elicited by the word "violence" should now be attached only to "illegal violence." "Legal violence," a much-used phrase of radicals, would have a meaning—law enforcement—but would no longer be reprehensible.

Many fringe radicals only commit violence because they have been confused by their gurus. The mere recital of obvious facts can, therefore, reduce their willingness to be violent. One cannot always convince people, especially those unaccustomed to thought, of even the most logical assertions. One can always, however, instill doubt in anyone whose mind is open. To some radicals, of course, radicalism is the psychic food without which they would founder into utter dejection. These dare not open their minds. The others—who constitute the majority of radicals—retain badly-oiled but intact rational faculties. If the vehemence of their self-righteous indignation can be reduced through reason, violence will diminish. Indeed, "vehemence of personal feeling . . . great ardor" is a secondary definition of "violence" (*Shorter Oxford English Dictionary*, 3rd edition).

The legitimacy of civil disobedience should be analyzed for the benefit of those committing it. It is a direct occasion of violence, for authorities are obliged to enforce the laws being violated. If radicals resist, violence is the inevitable outcome. To disobey the law with the intention of resisting arrest is therefore to seek violence.

The solution to violence is to remove its causes. As sloppy thinking is the cause of causes, the *sine qua non* of the other causes, clear thinking is the antidote. Violence is natural to people who have renounced the use of reason: if you do not believe in words, you must "act." On the intellectual level you make do with a handy slogan.

The vocabulary of the radical, for example, must be exposed as rhetorical. Radical oratory would be less convincing to undecided students if they were shown that when a radical says "legal violence," it usually means force properly used to protect our rights; that by "avoiding condescension" towards students, he means student power in the university; that by "simplistic" applied to the opposition, he means cogent, irrefutable; that by "legalistic" (which implies a lack of compassion), he means legal; that by "people," he means radicals; that by "participation," he means violence; and that by "democracy," he means radical dictatorship.

Radical stands on every issue should be dissected. The second chapter of this essay attempts to examine some of the principal radical clichés. Radicals are constantly using their slogans in new combinations, however, so that one absurdity can "prove" another. Concepts accepted by the general public are also mixed in. In order to establish the reparation principle, for example, black radicals bring in the popular old notion of collective guilt. What those desirous of peace must do is to take such a concept and examine all of its consequences. If collective guilt is a reasonable idea, for example, it follows that all Gentiles, including Negroes, are guilty of Auschwitz and Buchenwald. If all whites are guilty of slavery, so are all Negroes—for blacks were sold by fellow blacks. These hard verities must be discovered through reflection and spoken forthrightly. Students should eventually learn to discover them by themselves. This is what we mean by education.

The issues of each confrontation created by radicals should be thought out carefully; nothing should be done for expedience. It is impossible to calculate the harm done by professors who fear violence so much that they will do anything to avoid it. During the "People's Park" riots, the Berkeley Division of the Academic Senate adopted a resolution containing the following gem: "Since the continued presence of a fence around the entire lot is inappropriate to [a park] and is the immediate *cause* [my italics] of the intolerable physical conflict and police and military operations, . . . the fence around the park . . . [should be] removed." It is hard to believe that they did not see through this argument. Professors should be refuting rather than advancing such rot. Analyses blaming violence on fences around non-parks—because such fences are (supposedly) inappropriate to parks—are hardly going to restore rationality to the campuses of America. Even the premise that parks should not have fences is debatable. Many, in fact, do have them.

It is the relativism and anti-intellectualism of many university administrators which make them cynical about the effectiveness of reasoning. They do not believe that people can be convinced by argument and do not, therefore, avail themselves of the opportunities they are given to rebut radicals. Instead, they take above-the-fray airs and refuse to debate the issues. This is perhaps because they feel that the radicals are fools and that to debate with them would be to dignify their foolishness. Nevertheless, the result is that radicals doubt their own propaganda less and less. When administrators can no longer remain silent—after violence has occurred—they feel obliged to placate students and propose outlandish compromises. They should, rather, be presenting reasonable views on all the issues as often as possible. Professors and administrators have the primary responsibility to speak the truth, since their job is to seek and *disseminate* it. If they met this obligation, the one-sided debate would end. The sloppy radical thinking which causes violence would be largely neutralized.

Student non-radicals form a very large majority at present. Some students, more than their professors, are willing to speak out. At radical meetings supposedly devoted to free "dialogue," however, they are often deprived of the right to do so. The university should force the radicals to grant free speech at meetings on campus. This is the sort of cause which, morally, it must support, and which, tactically, it is wise to support. In violently protesting against free speech, radicals can only lose student support.

The student newspapers usually do publish all the letters sent to them. One administrator should have as his permanent chore the writing of rebuttals to the college newspaper. All of the nonsense in the preceding day's paper should be analyzed and refuted. This simple step would achieve a great deal. At present, there are very few non-radical letters sent. Campus newspapers are generally run by radicals for radicals.

There are many people to whom such suggestions will certainly appear comically naïve. Are rebuttals in college newspapers going to stop a violent mob? Is a discussion of words and ideas of any use in these times of hatred and mutual suspicion? What they fail to realize is that at the bottom of radicalism is nothing other than ideas. Remove the beliefs underpinning the radical movement and nothing is left but a number of young people with a strong desire for togetherness. This desire would never lead to self-righteous violence all by itself: it is the anti-Establishment beliefs which legitimize violence in the eyes of radicals. If ideas have caused violence, why should they not stop it?

This willingness to take certain ideas seriously—even if they are anti-intellectual ones—is the most endearing trait of radicals. They are often capable of going beyond what affects them personally. It is the opposite and most un-endearing trait of many non-radicals—a total disbelief in all ideas, combined with total absorption in their own situation in life—which makes them incapable of understanding the force of ideas in the world. They have, of course, been told that the French Revolution was prepared by the Enlightenment, that the Russian Revolution was prepared by Marx, that Auschwitz was prepared by Gobineau and by Nietzsche. They no doubt believed it. But when told that radicals *today* would not be radicals without at least an ideological framework, it is incomprehensible to them. Isn't all this talk about the corruption, racism, neocolonialism, and imperialism of America just so much talk? Aren't the real motives purely "emotional"? Isn't the radical's true wish simply to be in a crowd, to get drunk on rhetoric, to feel that he belongs to a movement?

To test this cynical view of events, let's suppose that Adolf Hitler, a great charismatic speaker, were to come to an American campus and give (in English) his best speeches. What influence would he have? The answer plainly indicates that ideas are here, as always, at the center of the problem. Hitler's ideas are out. Marcuse's are in. Is not the way to stop violence, then, to show how much Hitler and Marcuse have in common?

It may be concluded that the hard-boiled cynic, himself indifferent to ideas and supposing that the rest of mankind shares his toughness, is really the naïve soul in this case. He has failed to understand his adversary.

Professors and administrators should go beyond warding off radical attacks. They should—as individuals—present intelligent alternatives for student action. If radicals are demanding further preferential admissions for blacks, for example, they should compare such a program to one of their own. First, they would point out that using a lower admission standard for blacks is racism: it presupposes that equal opportunity is not enough for blacks, i.e., that they are inferior to American Chinese, Italians, Jews, and Irish. They would then propose something which would *truly* help eradicate racism, such as legally picketing unions which discriminate against blacks or circulating petitions to reduce the power of unions to discriminate. Between these two programs, one foolish and one sound, only the radicals themselves would choose the first. Without an alternative program, however, some sane people would adopt the first, harmful, idea because they would rather do anything than nothing at all.

Equally important, professors and administrators should not remain on the defensive. To be on the defensive is, in the public eye, to have a weaker case than the attacker. Everyone outside the university knows that the best of all defenses is a sharp offensive. Radicals, moreover, really make a much better target than the university: there are few groups more conformist, illogical, humorless, or totalitarian in America. The radical should be asked by open letter and in debate to justify some of the obvious contradictions between his opinions and his conduct. How, for example, does he explain his violence in the name of non-violence? How does he rationalize his living on an American economic level while supporting views which lead to levels three to ten times lower? How does he justify owning a car, that symbol of capitalist materialism? Automobiles make profits for American or other capitalist manufacturers and consequently produce tax monies for the support of war, imperialism, racism, and materialism. Every time he buys gasoline for it, he supports the "oil trusts" and supplies additional monies to capitalists and workers, all of whom pay into the war machine. He is also depleting natural resources, a major American sin in his opinion. In addition, there is not a single make of auto which does not have some parts made by a company which also makes war materiel.

One of his theses is that our high standard of living is due to the exploitation of blacks. Why then is he not actually giving most of his dirty American money to blacks? The greatest acts of financial sacrifice by radicals that have come to my attention are occurring in Madison, Wisconsin. At the Mifflin Street Community Grocery Cooperative, the poor are given a 6 percent discount! Is the radical an exploiter? Another tenet of his credo is that capitalists are evil because they wax fat on the labors of the proletariat while producing nothing themselves. Why then is the student radical not only unproductive but content to remain so? In short, why are his actions in total disaccord with his principles?

It is possible that there is an explanation. If he is obliged to give it, the psychology of events will be changed. He too will be judged and not only judge. He will no longer be part of a self-selected elite which attacks but is never obliged to defend itself. He may be so hard put to justify his behavior that he will begin to think. From that moment on, he will no longer be a violent radical.

When a radical contradicts himself, he should be asked to choose one of the two contradictory propositions and eliminate the other. When he has done this, he will retain very little ideology. If every time he contradicted himself it were pointed out, he would come to realize how foolish he is. In order to avoid contradiction, he would begin to think. That would be the end of radicalism as a major problem.

The peace-lover's goal is to remove emotional reactions and to replace them by reasoned ones (i.e., to educate). It is thus of prime importance not to eliminate academic requirements, selective admissions, grading, and work, which are essential ingredients of education. Let us change rather in the direction of solid instruction: more required courses, more total courses taken, more work in each course. Let us encourage more criticism from professors and more papers for students in which analysis is required. These papers must be judiciously corrected if the habit of reflection is to be instilled in students. The university, if it wants to make a useful reform, could lower the professor's course load and, in return, ask him to assign more papers and to correct and grade them himself.

The directed studies programs of the 1950's, in which students all took practically the same integrated curriculum during their first two years of college, were not only wise but "relevant." One of their goals was to show how various disciplines are connected and why in many cases they must nevertheless be treated as if they were not. Is this not the only serious answer to the complaint of irrelevance?

The presupposition of these programs was that professors could better judge what a student should study in his first two years of college than the student. Few graduates of such programs would *now* deny it. The present theory of complete liberty for the student is based on the opposite assumption. Radicals, of course, want both the relevance of directed studies and free choice. Had they taken a good program of directed studies, they would be less unreasonable.

In a word, violence will best be stopped by improving education, not by destroying it. In the long run, the very best thing the university can do to promote peace is to keep the educational machine going. It is not in a time of crisis that we should be tinkering with the mechanism. Changes made in passion are almost always for the worse. Those being proposed now, I have tried to show, are extremely dangerous. The simple refusal to change in radical directions would itself be a change in the right direction—and most useful to the university.

It has been stated that appeasement is a false solution to violence. The true solution is therefore to ignore what seems expedient, to do nothing hastily, to insist on some solid evidence that a change is desirable before making it, and to do nothing illegal (e.g., segregated programs or dormitories). Indeed the true solution is to punish illegal acts of any kind.

As the Bill of Rights is meaningless without laws forbidding certain acts (intimidation, violence) and therefore implies them, so these prohibitions imply enforcement. Enforcement is partially physical prevention: when students mass to take over a building, they can be dispersed. Physical prevention is really applicable, however, to very few crimes, for most illegal acts occur without warning. The students gathered on the steps of a building may merely be indulging in legal protest. Enforcement, therefore, usually takes the form of punishment. The law is enforced—as best it can be—by the knowledge on the part of the potential criminal that if caught, he will pay for it.

Most societies give punishment a double role. It is seen as a deterrent to crime and as revenge. Few Americans believe in the eye for an eye type of justice these days. It is the theory of deterrence alone which justifies punishment in the American mind. To most professional educators, however, the argument that threat of punishment deters crime is old-fashioned and false. They have read in countless socio-psychological studies that punishment is more likely to cause morbid interest in crime than a healthy fear of it. One hears statistics quoted to the effect that in Wagaluma County, Illinois, the murder rate went down by 3.1 per cent after the death penalty was removed.

"Science" has demolished the case for deterrence. Consequently, the very word "punishment" evokes horror in the university man. Punishment is "repression." It is a "fascist tactic."

It makes those subjected to it compulsive, sadistic, inhuman, and generally sick. Had these same people been treated with Love, they would now all be good citizens.

This theory has its hidden suppositions, the first of which is that sociological studies are a better source of truth than reason. The second is that criminals are not really like you and me. For if they were, and if reason were a legitimate means of discovering truth, we could simply look into our own hearts to find out whether threat of punishment is a deterrent to crime.

Let us refuse for a moment the quasi-racist assumption that humanity is divided into good folk like us and the "criminal element." In that case, we can ask ourselves why we do not cheat on our income taxes or shoplift. After all, we could always find some rationalization to salve our consciences. We could say, for example, that taxes pay for war, and that merchants exploit the people. Any sort of pap will do. But that handcuff, that news item, that prison sentence—that is another matter. Empirical proof that fear of punishment prevents crime is no more difficult to obtain than rational proof. October 7, 1969 was the worst day of lawlessness in the history of the city of Montreal. October 7, 1969 was also the day on which the city's 3,700 policemen went out on strike.

The honest use of sense experience and reason thus tells us very clearly that punishment is a very effective deterrent for Montrealers and for us. What of radicals? A bit of propaganda circulated at the University of California, Berkeley during the "People's Park" rioting, and signed "POWER TO THE PEOPLE," contains an indication that even brave revolutionaries can be deterred by the threat of punishment: "Today at noon there is a rally in Sproul Plaza to begin this week's offensive. After the rally, we will go down Shattuck [Avenue] and picket merchants who do not support us. The concept on Shattuck is to be linear: not to form crowds, but to mill and picket. This will close off the street. This is a perfectly legal act." This last sentence should reassure those who fear that radicals are a new race. Why are people who have illegally seized a vacant lot concerned with legality? Why are those sworn to the destruction of laws "made by the pigs" careful not to commit an infraction? Only the fear of punishment is a likely explanation. Why risk punishment if you can "close off the street" without doing so?

During a session of picketing military recruiters at the University of California at Davis, SDS and Resistance leaders offered two plans to their followers. The first, as reported by the *California Aggie* of May 16, 1969, was as follows:

". . . 'recruiters might be escorted off campus and their material confiscated, in which case there may be a chance that participants might be arrested for assault and battery, and suffer disciplinary action by the University,' said one organizer from SDS.

" 'Furthermore, under the first plan, non-students participating in this action would be prosecuted under the Mulford Act,' which provides very stiff penalties.

"The second plan suggested by the demonstration organizers involved inundating the porch to prevent persons from speaking to recruiters, in which case 'we may be arrested for trespassing.'

"A hand count was taken and the latter suggestion won general approval."

The penalty for trespassing is, of course, a very light one. Much greater violence would have been committed had it not been for the fear of punishment.

This brings us to a generalization from which there are a few, but very few exceptions: when the legitimate power of an organization (university, state, grouping of states) decreases, but before it has been replaced by despotism, violence increases. The feeling that there is no real power anywhere pervades the university, especially the large university. This impression is, of course, false. Someone does make decisions. In a given case, however, very few know who it is. The tendency of administrators to pass the buck encourages this ignorance. In addition, power rarely punishes. The solution is to restore the awareness that there is a legal authority which can and does punish.

The fact that laws exist which are not applied has made many people feel that in the larger community as well, one runs little real risk of being punished. A muddled but very sincere Teaching Assistant with whom I am acquainted had decided he could not serve the military machine. He wrote his draft board explaining his position and announcing his willingness to be punished. He was perfectly convinced of his honesty. When some eight months later he received a visit from a government official, he was astonished. He always knew he could be punished, he told me, but it had never seemed "real" before! Without realizing it, he had discounted the possibility of punishment *before* making his noble gesture. The dictates of his conscience might have been less imperative had he really been certain of receiving punishment. His initial feeling, incidentally, was right, for in the two years that have passed since this incident, he has not been prosecuted.

The restoration of power in the university could be brought about very simply. The academic senate would pass rules accompanied by a list of the punishments for disobeying them. We already have some rules, of course, but they are so vaguely worded that nobody can say with absolute certainty of an act, "This is forbidden," unless it is assault and battery or murder which is being discussed. And punishments are not listed. It should be made clear in this student penal code that all crimes committed against municipal, state or federal laws are the concern of those governments. The university would *automatically* sign all complaints when it was the injured party. It would make no attempt to protect its violent students. Those days, alas, can be no more. The university must now protect itself, i.e., those who sincerely wish to teach, to learn, or both.

Infractions of university rules must of course be dealt with by the university. There should be as little leeway for bargaining on punishments as is feasible. Under the present vague rules, a given offense can go unpunished or lead to expulsion from the university. Power that should be in university *law* belongs rather to a few university *people*. University government consequently is all influence, expedience, fear, and tyranny. The rule of law is so much simpler and better. John Jones strikes his professor. He is expelled automatically because the university law 523 states unequivocally that striking professors leads to expulsion whether John Jones is white or black, whether he is radical or liberal, and whether the professor forgives him or not. Whether John Jones is also prosecuted publicly for assault and battery is up to the professor. The instructor at Columbia who was struck in the face by a radical student wielding a wooden board would probably have welcomed such a rule.

It is especially important that university rules be clear and detailed. If they do not cover most situations imaginable, they are useless. They must be widely disseminated. University libraries often oblige students borrowing books to sign a card pledging that they will obey library rules. One could simply put all rules on a piece of paper and have the student sign his promise to obey them at registration time. He could keep a carbon copy for his scrapbook. Those unwilling to promise obedience would not be allowed to register. Student rights would be defined by the same token: students would be allowed to do anything not forbidden by university, municipal, state, or federal laws. This document would further state that the university, far from wishing to stifle dissent, actively *seeks* it. Disagreement and dissent are in no way related to lawlessness. Since the obvious sometimes escapes students, there is no harm in pointing out that certain actions can and should be forbidden, but that speech is free.

It should go without saying, since laws imply law enforcement, that the university should have plans for all contingencies. The local police should confer with universities before, not during, crises. The degree of force required in a given situation should be decided upon. When trouble begins, a well-oiled machinery of defense should be available.

Policemen who violate the law by committing assault and battery should be treated like any other criminals. They too should know clearly what is allowed and what is not. Police photographers should be on hand in all riots. Performances should be reviewed the following day—as with football teams. If, as the police say, the press shows pictures of policemen hitting radicals but rarely of radicals attacking policemen, these pictures would be proof. They would also aid in the prosecution of the guilty.

Does this mean that the day such proposals were adopted peace would reign? In fact, on a very short-term basis, it could mean more violence. Radicals would hope to resist such measures by violence, not only because it is their "thing," but because it would prove, by its mere existence, that the recipe is wrong!

After it became crystal clear to all that *nothing* could be gained by brutishness, however (not because administrators were saying so, but because, in fact, a certain period of time would have passed without a single concession being made to the violent), violence would diminish. After it became a certitude that the individual committing violence would, in fact, lose something, that he would be punished, violence would cease.

Finally, if students came to understand the causes of violence, its usual results, and the issues involved in the present violence—if they became educated—the very desire for violent action against the university would disappear.